MW01181540

VENICE
TRAVEL GUIDE
2018

SHOPS, RESTAURANTS, *ATTRACTIONS* & *NIGHTLIFE*

The Most Positively
Reviewed and Recommended
by Locals and Travelers

EGP
Editorial

VENICE
TRAVEL GUIDE
2018

SHOPS, RESTAURANTS, ATTRACTIONS & NIGHTLIFE

VENICE TRAVEL GUIDE 2018
Shops, Restaurants, Attractions & Nightlife

© Herbert R. Garris, 2018
© E.G.P. Editorial, 2018

ISBN-13: 978-1545011386
ISBN-10: 1545011389

INDEX

VENICE TRAVEL GUIDE 2018
Shops, Restaurants, Attractions & Nightlife

*This directory is dedicated to Venice Business Owners and Managers
who provide the experience that the locals and tourists enjoy.
Thanks you very much for all that you do and thank for being the "People Choice".*

*Thanks to everyone that posts their reviews online and
the amazing reviews sites that make our life easier.*

*The places listed in this book are the most positively reviewed
and recommended by locals and travelers from around the world.*

*Thank you for your time and enjoy the directory that is
designed with locals and tourist in mind!*

TOP 500 SHOPS
The Most Recommended by Locals & Trevelers
(From #1 to #500)

#1
Teatro La Fenice
Category: Music & DVDs
Address: Campo San Fantin 1965
30124 Venezia Italy
Phone: +39 04 1786511

#2
**Libreria Acqua Alta
di Frizzo Luigi**
Category: Bookstore
Address: Sestiere Castello 5167
30122 Venezia Italy
Phone: +39 04 12960841

#3
Il Grifone
Category: Luggage
Address: Fondamenta del Gaffaro 3516
30123 Venezia Italy
Phone: +39 04 15229452

#4
CA' Macana
Category: Arts & Crafts
Address: Sestiere Dorsoduro, 3172
30123 Venezia Italy
Phone: +39 04 15203229

#5
Palazzo Grassi
Category: Art Gallery
Address: 3231 Campo San Samuele
30124 Venezia Italy
Phone: +39 04 15236180

#6
Murano Venetian Glass Center
Category: Art Gallery
Address: Calle San Cipriano 48
30100 Venezia Italy
Phone: +39 04 1736894

#7
Aqua Alta
Category: Fashion
Address: Via Cannaregio, 5690
30131 Venezia Italy
Phone: +39 04 15231466

#8
Coop. Adriatica Soc. Coop. ARL
Category: Shopping Center, Grocery
Address: Sestiere Castello, 5989
30122 Venezia Italy
Phone: +39 04 15223415

#9
L'Isola
Category: Flowers & Gifts, Art Gallery
Address: Sestiere San Marco 1468
30124 Venezia Italy
Phone: +39 04 15231973

#10
La Bottega dei Mascareri
Category: Arts & Crafts
Address: Sestiere San Polo 80
30125 Venezia Italy
Phone: +39 04 15223857

#11
Fabricharte
Category: Cards & Stationery
Address: San Marco 2511
30124 Venezia Italy
Phone: +39 327 4972022

#12
Fiorella Gallery
Category: Art Gallery
Address: Campo Santo Stefano 2806
30124 Venezia Italy
Phone: +39 06 3203500

#13
Burberry Italy Retail
Category: Accessories, Men's Clothing,
Women's Clothing
Address: Sestiere San Marco 2308
30124 Venezia Italy
Phone: +39 04 1240291

#14
Bauledoriente
Category: Jewelry
Address: Sestiere Cannaregio 190
30121 Venezia Italy
Phone: +39 04 15201362

#15
De Laurentis Glass
Category: Home Decor
Address: Dorsodoro 2766/A
30123 Venezia Italy
Phone: +39 04 15280195

#16
CA' Macana Atelier
di Brassesco & Vicente
Category: Home & Garden
Address: Sestiere Cannaregio, 1374
30131 Venezia Italy
Phone: +39 04 1718655

#17
Cose cosi
Category: Jewelry
Address: Fondamenta Manin 75 A
30141 Venezia Italy
Phone: +39 04 1739780

#18
Louis Vuitton
Category: Fashion
Address: 1345 San Marco
30124 Venezia Italy
Phone: +39 390 415224500

#19
MM Venezia
Category: Fabric Store
Address: Calle Larga G Gallina 6376
30121 Venezia Italy
Phone: +39 04 15210019

#20
Dunia Shop di TAN Teong Chiew
Category: Fashion
Address: Sestiere S. Marco, 4341
30124 Venezia Italy
Phone: +39 04 15237267

#21
Zanutto Vincenzo
Category: Antiques
Address: Via Sestiere San Marco
30124 Venezia Italy
Phone: +39 04 15235359

#22
Libreria Giunti AL Punto
Category: Bookstore
Address: Sestiere SAN Polo, 1128
30125 Venezia Italy
Phone: +39 04 15208760

#23
Atelier Marega
Category: Costumes
Address: Campo San Rocco 3046A
30122 Venezia Italy
Phone: +39 04 15221634

#24
Giudecca Art Gallery 795
Category: Art Gallery
Address: Fondamenta San Biagio 795
Giudecca, 30133 Venezia Italy
Phone: +39 04 17241182

#25
Profumeria Franco
Category: Cosmetics & Beauty Supply
Address: Sestiere S. Marco, 5333
30124 Venezia Italy
Phone: +39 04 15226307

#26
Murano Glass Factories
Category: Home Decor
Address: Castello 4623
30122 Venezia Italy
Phone: +39 04 12412202

#27
Ponte De Rialto
Category: Gift Shop
Address: 30125 Venezia Italy
Phone: +39 04 12748111

#28
Sephora Italia
Category: Cosmetics & Beauty Supply
Address: Sestiere Cannaregio 5783
30121 Venezia Italy
Phone: +39 04 15231995

#29
Shiraz
Category: Flowers & Gifts, Home Decor
Address: Via Fondamenta Della Misericorsia
Cannaredio 2573
30100 Venezia Italy
Phone: +39 04 1740108

#30
Lala
Category: Jewelry
Address: San Marco 719
30124 Venezia Italy
Phone: +39 04 15286517

#31
Lush Shop
Category: Cosmetics & Beauty Supply
Address: Cannaregio, Strada Nuova 3822
30121 Venezia Italy
Phone: +39 04 12411200

#32
Pantalon 47 di Laura Venier
Category: Arts & Crafts
Address: Sestiere S. Croce, 47
30135 Venezia Italy
Phone: +39 04 15244147

#33
Cartoleria Accademia
Category: Cards & Stationery
Address: Sestiere Dorsoduro, 1007/A
30123 Venezia Italy
Phone: +39 04 15285283

#34
Lush Italia
Category: Cosmetics & Beauty Supply
Address: Sestiere Cannaregio 3822
30131 Venezia Italy
Phone: +39 04 12411200

#35
H & M Hennes & Mauritz
Category: Fashion
Address: Campo San Luca 4473C
30124 Venezia Italy
Phone: +39 04 12413165

#36
Coop. Adriatica
Category: Shopping Center, Grocery
Address: Sestiere San Croce
30135 Venezia Italy
Phone: +39 04 12960621

#37
I Love Tourism Shop
Category: Fashion
Address: S.Marco 71/c
30124 Venezia Italy
Phone: +39 04 15237819

#38
Libreria La Toletta
Category: Bookstore
Address: Dorsoduro 1213
30100 Venezia Italy
Phone: +39 04 15232034

#39
Giorgio Nason
Category: Arts & Crafts
Address: Dorsoduro 167
30123 Venezia Italy
Phone: +39 04 15239426

#40
Ganesha Gems of Venice
Category: Jewelry
Address: San Polo 1044
30125 Venezia Italy
Phone: +39 00 390415225148

#41
Il Tempio Della Musica Simone
Category: Vinyl Records
Address: Via San Marco 5368
30124 Venezia Italy
Phone: +39 04 15234552

#42
**Libreria Al Capitello
di Federica Pozzi**
Category: Bookstore
Address: Via Cannaregio 3762
30121 Venezia Italy
Phone: +39 04 15222314

#43
Billa AG
Category: Shopping Center, Grocery
Address: Sestiere Dorsoduro 1491
30100 Venezia Italy
Phone: +39 04 15226187

#44
Billa
Category: Discount Store
Address: Gran Viale S. M. Elisabetta
30123 Venezia Italy
Phone: +39 04 15262898

#45
Moleskine
Category: Office Equipment
Address: Stazione Santa Lucia
30121 Venezia Italy
Phone: +39 04 1740913

#46
Galleria Ca' Rezzonico
Category: Art Gallery
Address: Via Sestiere Di Dorsoduro 2793
30123 Venezia Italy
Phone: +39 04 15280035

#47
Charme Profumeria / Silvia
Category: Cosmetics & Beauty Supply
Address: Via Dorsoduro, 1183/B
30123 Venezia Italy
Phone: +39 04 15238691

#48
The Merchant of Venice
Category: Perfume
Address: Campo San Fantin 1895
30124 Venezia Italy
Phone: +39 04 12960559

#49
Atelier Flavia
Category: Souvenir Shop, Costumes
Address: Castello, 6010
30122 Venezia Italy
Phone: +39 04 15287429

#50
DMM
Category: Computers
Address: Via Castello 3385E
30122 Venezia Italy
Phone: +39 04 12770143

#51
Trevisin / Germana
Category: Fashion
Address: Sestiere Dorsoduro, 1189
30123 Venezia Italy
Phone: +39 04 15285752

#52
Mud&Water store
Category: Fashion, Music & DVDs
Address: Sestiere San Polo 51
30125 Venezia Italy
Phone: +39 04 15220829

#53
Foto Ottica Paties Bruno
Category: Eyewear & Opticians
Address: Via Sestiere Castello 1738
30122 Venezia Italy
Phone: +39 04 15231620

#54
Viani Nadia
Category: Art Gallery
Address: Via Dorsoduro, 1195
30123 Venezia Italy
Phone: +39 04 15223159

#55
Libreria Tarantola Bruno
Category: Bookstore
Address: Sestiere San Marco 4268
30124 Venezia Italy
Phone: +39 04 15223413

#56
Ninfea Arte e Bijoux
Category: Jewelry
Address: Castello 5228
30122 Venezia Italy
Phone: +39 04 15210072

#57
Livio De Marchi
Category: Arts & Crafts
Address: Salizzada San Samuele 3157/a
30124 Venezia Italy
Phone: +39 04 15285694

#58
Gruppo Coin
Category: Shopping Center, Grocery,
Department Store
Address: Sestiere Cannaregio 5788
30131 Venezia Italy
Phone: +39 04 15203581

#59
La Pedrera
Category: Jewelry
Address: Sestiere SAN Polo, 2279/A
30125 Venezia Italy
Phone: +39 04 12440144

#60
Solesin Matteo
Category: Tobacco Shop
Address: Isola della Giudecca 37
30133 Venezia Italy
Phone: +39 04 12410589

#61
Ferrari / Pasquale
Category: Musical Instruments
Address: Sestiere Castello, 4369
30122 Venezia Italy
Phone: +39 04 15230170

#62
Ad un passo dai Miracoli
Category: Lighting Fixtures & Equipment,
Home Decor, Furniture Store
Address: San Marco 4865
30124 Venezia Italy
Phone: +39 333 6630652

#63
Fanfaluca di Buttner Nedjma
Category: Toy Store, Luggage
Address: Sestiere S. Croce, 779
30135 Venezia Italy
Phone: +39 04 15287103

#64
**Libreria Editrice
Cafoscarina S.P.A.**
Category: Bookstore
Address: Sestiere Dorsoduro 3224
30100 Venezia Italy
Phone: +39 04 15231814

#65
Ottica Paties
Category: Eyewear & Opticians
Address: Via Garibaldi Castello 1738 31030
Venezia Italy
Phone: +39 04 15231620

#66
Wonderland
Category: Books, Mags, Music & Video
Address: Calle dei Botteri 1573
30125 Venezia Italy
Phone: +39 04 1721173

#67
**Libreria AL Milion
di Filippi Luciano**
Category: Bookstore
Address: Sestiere Castello 5763
30122 Venezia Italy
Phone: +39 04 15235635

#68
Marciana
Category: Antiques
Address: Sestiere S. Marco, 1864
30124 Venezia Italy
Phone: +39 04 15235666

#69
Mare
Category: Fashion
Address: Sestiere S. Marco, 218
30124 Venezia Italy
Phone: +39 04 15205631

#70
**Boutique Giorgio Armani
di Sartori Simonetta**
Category: Fashion
Address: Sestiere S. Marco, 4412
30124 Venezia Italy
Phone: +39 04 15234758

#71
D&G Dolce & Gabbana Boutique
Category: Fashion
Address: Sestiere S. Marco, 712
30124 Venezia Italy
Phone: +39 04 12960502

#72
**Luna Creazioni
di Daros Annabella**
Category: Antiques
Address: Sestiere S. Marco, 1850
30124 Venezia Italy
Phone: +39 04 15238006

#73
Boudoir Galleria Ottica
Category: Eyewear & Opticians
Address: Dorsoduro 2751
30123 Venezia Italy
Phone: +39 04 12410192

#74
La Foglia D'oro S.A.S.
Category: Jewelry
Address: Sestiere SAN Polo, 2768/C
30125 Venezia Italy
Phone: +39 04 1714742

#75
L'Arlecchino
Category: Arts & Crafts
Address: Sestiere San Polo 789
30125 Venezia Italy
Phone: +39 04 15208220

#76
Ganesha di Cook Angela Jane
Category: Oriental Goods
Address: Sestiere SAN Polo, 1044
30125 Venezia Italy
Phone: +39 04 15225148

#77
**Coop. Adriatica Soc.
Coop. ARL Centralino**
Category: Shopping Center, Grocery
Address: Sestiere Castello 6576
30122 Venezia Italy
Phone: +39 04 12412462

#78
Nardi / Francesco Neri
Category: Antiques
Address: Sestiere Castello, 4867
30122 Venezia Italy
Phone: +39 04 12413122

#79
Farmacia Dott.ssa
Laura Perissinotto
Category: Drugstore
Address: Via Cannaregio 4437
30121 Venezia Italy
Phone: +39 04 15224239

#80
Itaca Art Studio di Martin Monica
Category: Art Gallery
Address: Sestiere Castello 5267A
30122 Venezia Italy
Phone: +39 04 15203207

#81
Foto Ottica Viani
Category: Eyewear & Opticians
Address: Sestiere Cannaregio 5755
30121 Venezia Italy
Phone: +39 04 15228095

#82
Ragazzi / Marino
Category: Arts & Crafts
Address: Sestiere Castello, 5792
30122 Venezia Italy
Phone: +39 04 15221903

#83
Biennale Di Venezia Giardini
Category: Art Gallery
Address: Calle Paludo
30122 Venezia Italy
Phone: +39 04 15218711

#84
Coop. Adriatica Soc. Coop. ARL
Category: Shopping Center, Grocery
Address: cannaregio 1976
30121 Venezia Italy
Phone: +39 04 1720374

#85
Libreria Editrice Filippi
Category: Bookstore
Address: Sestiere Castello 5284
30122 Venezia Italy
Phone: +39 04 15236916

#86
Verrerie Mazzega
Category: Arts & Crafts
Address: Venezia Italy
Phone: +39 04 1736888

#87
Farmacia Alle Due Colonne E S.
Category: Drugstore
Address: Via Cannaregio 6045
30121 Venezia Italy
Phone: +39 04 15225411

#88
Magie di Carnevale
Category: Arts & Crafts
Address: Salizada San Provolo Castello
4518 30122 Venezia Italy
Phone: +39 04 15227310

#89
Libreria Miracoli
di Vascon Claudio
Category: Bookstore
Address: Sestiere Cannaregio, 6062
30131 Venezia Italy
Phone: +39 04 15234060

#90
ItaliaGid
Category: Tours, Personal Shopping
Address: 30124 Venezia Italy
Phone: +39 339 1792600

#91
Glass Dream
Category: Arts & Crafts
Address: San Marco 633
30124 Venezia Italy
Phone: +39 04 15228589

#92
LT2
Category: Bookstore
Address: Sestiere Dorsoduro, 1183/D
30123 Venezia Italy
Phone: +39 04 15229481

#93
Coop. Adriatica Soc. Coop. ARL
Category: Shopping Center, Grocery
Address: Sestiere SAN Polo, 1338/A
30125 Venezia Italy
Phone: +39 04 15232288

#94
Capogiro di Vardanega Riccardo
Category: Fashion
Address: Sestiere Castello, 3913
30122 Venezia Italy
Phone: +39 04 15229955

#95
Coop. Adriatica Soc. Coop. ARL
Category: Shopping Center, Grocery
Address: Sestiere S. Croce, 1493
30135 Venezia Italy
Phone: +39 04 12750218

#96
Gucci Store
Category: Fashion
Address: Mercerie dell'orologio - San Marco
258 Venezia Italy
Phone: +39 444 12413968

#97
Occhi di Gatto
Category: Gift Shop, Souvenir Shop
Address: Castello N. 4124
30122 Venezia Italy
Phone: +39 04 15231175

#98
Lala
Category: Jewelry
Address: Cannaregio 4290
30121 Venezia Italy
Phone: +39 04 15237795

#99
Giovanna Zanella
Category: Shoe Store, Leather Goods
Address: San Lio 30122 Venezia Italy
Phone: +39 04 15235500

#100
Gavagnin Roberto
Category: Fashion
Address: Piazza SAN Marco, 4364
30124 Venezia Italy
Phone: +39 04 12410937

#101
L'arte Della Carta
Category: Cards & Stationery
Address: Piazza SAN Marco, 1179
30124 Venezia Italy
Phone: +39 04 15202257

#102
Laura Crovato / Laura
Category: Fashion
Address: Piazza SAN Marco, 2995
30124 Venezia Italy
Phone: +39 04 15204170

#103
Edicola S.Luca di M.
Category: Newspapers & Magazines
Address: Piazza SAN Marco, 4156/B
30124 Venezia Italy
Phone: +39 04 15228174

#104
Antoniamiletto
Category: Jewelry
Address: Piazza S.marco, 3208/A
30124 Venezia Italy
Phone: +39 04 15205177

#105
Caos Nicola
Category: Art Gallery
Address: Piazza San Marco 1047
30124 Venezia Italy
Phone: +39 04 12413561

#106
Aliseo
Category: Jewelry
Address: Via Sestiere SAN Marco, 365
30100 Venezia Italy
Phone: +39 04 15235695

#107
Calzature Lions di Paviola E.
Category: Shoe Store
Address: Via Sestiere S. Croce, 554
30170 Venezia Italy
Phone: +39 04 15231542

#108
La Soffitta
Category: Antiques
Address: Sestiere Dorsoduro, 3488/C
30123 Venezia Italy
Phone: +39 04 1710211

#109
Marazzi / Loris
Category: Art Gallery
Address: Sestiere Dorsoduro, 369
30123 Venezia Italy
Phone: +39 04 15239001

#110
Massarolli / Michele
Category: Tobacco Shop
Address: Sestiere Dorsoduro, 1640
30123 Venezia Italy
Phone: +39 04 15231456

#111
Micheluzzi / Massimo
Category: Antiques
Address: Sestiere Dorsoduro, 1071
30123 Venezia Italy
Phone: +39 04 15282190

#112
Nadia
Category: Leather Goods
Address: Sestiere Dorsoduro, 2762
30123 Venezia Italy
Phone: +39 04 15228677

#113
Galleria D'arte L'occhio
Category: Art Gallery
Address: Sestiere Dorsoduro, 181
30123 Venezia Italy
Phone: +39 04 15226550

#114
**La Vispa Teresa SNC
di Memo Marianna**
Category: Fashion
Address: Sestiere Dorsoduro, 3701
30123 Venezia Italy
Phone: +39 04 15204463

#115
Marina e Susanna Sent
Category: Jewelry
Address: Sestiere Dorsoduro, 681
30123 Venezia Italy
Phone: +39 04 15238817

#116
**Antichita' Pietro Scarpa
di Pietro Scarpa**
Category: Antiques
Address: Sestiere Dorsoduro, 1023
30123 Venezia Italy
Phone: +39 04 15239700

#117
Baga Shop di Bagarotto Fabio
Category: Tobacco Shop
Address: Sestiere Dorsoduro, 865
30123 Venezia Italy
Phone: +39 04 15237222

#118
Cartoleria Accademia
Category: Cards & Stationery
Address: Sestiere Dorsoduro, 1044
30123 Venezia Italy
Phone: +39 04 15207086

#119
Enrico Ansevini
Category: Tobacco Shop
Address: Sestiere Dorsoduro, 2387
30123 Venezia Italy
Phone: +39 04 12750470

#120
**Genninger Studio
di Genninger Leslie ANN**
Category: Jewelry
Address: Sestiere Dorsoduro, 364
30123 Venezia Italy
Phone: +39 04 15225565

#121
**Bressanello ART Studio
di Bressanello Fabio**
Category: Art Gallery
Address: Sestiere Dorsoduro, 2835/A
30123 Venezia Italy
Phone: +39 04 17241080

#122
Dittura Massimo
Category: Shoe Store
Address: Sestiere Dorsoduro, 871
30123 Venezia Italy
Phone: +39 04 15231163

#123
Donini Beatrice
Category: Cards & Stationery
Address: Sestiere Dorsoduro, 3954
30123 Venezia Italy
Phone: +39 04 15203710

#124
Libreria del Campo SAS
di Ancely Tristano
Category: Bookstore
Address: Sestiere Dorsoduro, 2943
30123 Venezia Italy
Phone: +39 04 15210624

#125
Papuni ART di Ninfa Salerno
Category: Jewelry
Address: Sestiere Dorsoduro, 2834/A
30123 Venezia Italy
Phone: +39 04 12410434

#126
Casin dei Nobili Show Room SNC di
Oliani Stefano e Valentina
Category: Party Supplies,
Arts & Crafts, Flowers & Gifts
Address: Sestiere Dorsoduro, 2766
30123 Venezia Italy
Phone: +39 04 15202873

#127
DE Gaspari
Category: Cards & Stationery
Address: Sestiere Dorsoduro, 3522
30123 Venezia Italy
Phone: +39 04 1717135

#128
Bacci Gregorio
Category: Art Gallery
Address: Sestiere Dorsoduro 720B
30123 Venezia Italy
Phone: +39 04 15287934

#129
Fornari / Ermellina
Category: Tobacco Shop
Address: Sestiere Dorsoduro, 2768
30123 Venezia Italy
Phone: +39 04 15236088

#130
LT2
Category: Bookstore
Address: Sestiere Dorsoduro, 1134
30123 Venezia Italy
Phone: +39 04 15208194

#131
Rava' Tobia
Category: Art Gallery
Address: Sestiere Dorsoduro 2324
30123 Venezia Italy
Phone: +39 04 12750332

#132
Antiquus
Category: Antiques
Address: Sestiere Dorsoduro, 873/A
30123 Venezia Italy
Phone: +39 04 12413725

#133
Cartoleria SAN Trovaso
di Luigi Gianola
Category: Cards & Stationery
Address: Sestiere Dorsoduro, 1077
30123 Venezia Italy
Phone: +39 04 15223071

#134
Rubelli / Elvira
Category: Leather Goods
Address: Sestiere Dorsoduro, 3749
30123 Venezia Italy
Phone: +39 04 1720595

#135
Albarea / Barbara
Category: Tobacco Shop
Address: Sestiere Dorsoduro, 791
30123 Venezia Italy
Phone: +39 04 15207605

#136
Grandesso / Antonio
Category: Tobacco Shop
Address: Sestiere Dorsoduro, 2979
30123 Venezia Italy
Phone: +39 04 15227721

#137
Ikona Photo Gallery
Category: Art Gallery
Address: Sestiere Dorsoduro 48
30123 Venezia Italy
Phone: +39 04 15205854

#138
Salata / Giampietro
Category: Jewelry
Address: Sestiere Dorsoduro, 3928
30123 Venezia Italy
Phone: +39 04 15237135

#139
Soffiato / Ivano
Category: Arts & Crafts
Address: Sestiere Dorsoduro, 1188
30123 Venezia Italy
Phone: +39 04 15210480

#140
Shanti Daan Di S.N.C.
di A. Ferro E S. Campana
Category: Oriental Goods
Address: Sestiere Dorsoduro, 3284
30123 Venezia Italy
Phone: +39 04 12411916

#141
Zocchia Luigi
Category: Leather Goods
Address: Sestiere Dorsoduro, 3855/B
30123 Venezia Italy
Phone: +39 04 15223910

#142
MAX Studio
Category: Art Gallery
Address: Sestiere Dorsoduro 1053C
30123 Venezia Italy
Phone: +39 04 15227773

#143
San Gregorio Art Gallery
Category: Art Gallery
Address: Sestiere Dorsoduro 164
30123 Venezia Italy
Phone: +39 04 15229296

#144
Trasparenze S.A.S.
Category: Flowers & Gifts
Address: Sestiere Dorsoduro, 190
30123 Venezia Italy
Phone: +39 04 12774427

#145
Videomat Service
di Giove Marzia
Category: Videos & Video Game Rental
Address: Sestiere Dorsoduro, 3683
30123 Venezia Italy
Phone: +39 04 15227960

#146
Cartoleria A.D. Arte & Design
Category: Cards & Stationery
Address: Sestiere Dorsoduro, 2408
30123 Venezia Italy
Phone: +39 04 1718898

#147
L'angolo del Passato
di Naccari Giordana
Category: Antiques
Address: Sestiere Dorsoduro, 3276/A
30123 Venezia Italy
Phone: +39 04 15287896

#148
LT2
Category: Bookstore
Address: Sestiere Dorsoduro, 1214
30123 Venezia Italy
Phone: +39 04 15232034

#149
Vignotto / Maria
Category: Tobacco Shop
Address: Sestiere Dorsoduro, 1015
30123 Venezia Italy
Phone: +39 04 15236663

#150
C'era UNA Volta
Category: Cards & Stationery
Address: Sestiere Dorsoduro, 3739
30123 Venezia Italy
Phone: +39 04 1718899

#151
Elettronautica Veneziana
di Vianello Pierluigi
Category: Sporting Goods
Address: Sestiere Dorsoduro, 298
30123 Venezia Italy
Phone: +39 04 15231073

#152
Ferruzzi Roberto
Category: Art Gallery
Address: Sestiere Dorsoduro 523
30123 Venezia Italy
Phone: +39 04 15228582

#153
Tiozzo / Mauro
Category: Tobacco Shop
Address: Sestiere Dorsoduro, 2120
30123 Venezia Italy
Phone: +39 04 15207340

#154
Vianello / Nazareno
Category: Cards & Stationery
Address: Sestiere Dorsoduro, 2759
30123 Venezia Italy
Phone: +39 04 12770926

#155
Autoscuola Fiume
Category: Sporting Goods,
Driving School
Address: Sestiere S. Marco, 4827
30124 Venezia Italy
Phone: +39 04 15287108

#156
Antichita' Pietro Scarpa
Category: Antiques
Address: Sestiere S. Marco, 44
30124 Venezia Italy
Phone: +39 04 12960291

#157
Barovier Marino
Category: Art Gallery
Address: Sestiere S. Marco, 3202
30124 Venezia Italy
Phone: +39 04 15236748

#158
Boncompagni / Icilio
Category: Jewelry
Address: Sestiere S. Marco, 131/132
30124 Venezia Italy
Phone: +39 04 15224563

#159
Cosmo SAS di Lanza Matteo
Category: Flowers & Gifts
Address: Sestiere S. Marco, 801
30124 Venezia Italy
Phone: +39 04 15231332

#160
Dolfin Daniela
Category: Antiques
Address: Sestiere S. Marco, 3661
30124 Venezia Italy
Phone: +39 04 15203283

#161
**Gioielleria Seno Luciano
di Donaggio Marina**
Category: Home Decor
Address: Sestiere S. Marco, 5215
30124 Venezia Italy
Phone: +39 04 15205292

#162
Giordan
Category: Jewelry
Address: Sestiere S. Marco, 78/C
30124 Venezia Italy
Phone: +39 04 15224289

#163
**La Carta S.N.C.
di Vianello Elio**
Category: Flowers & Gifts
Address: Sestiere S. Marco, 5547/A
30124 Venezia Italy
Phone: +39 04 15202325

#164
**Italosport ONE SAS
di Traverso Giampaolo**
Category: Sporting Goods
Address: Sestiere S. Marco, 4254
30124 Venezia Italy
Phone: +39 04 15200696

#165
La Ricerca
Category: Cards & Stationery
Address: Sestiere S. Marco, 2236
30124 Venezia Italy
Phone: +39 04 15228250

#166
Luxury Goods Italia
Category: Fashion
Address: Sestiere S. Marco, 258
30124 Venezia Italy
Phone: +39 04 12412194

#167
Masnagotre
Category: Men's Clothing
Address: Sestiere S. Marco, 4844
30124 Venezia Italy
Phone: +39 04 15237733

#168
Mattiuzzi / Pietro
Category: Jewelry
Address: Sestiere S. Marco, 788
30124 Venezia Italy
Phone: +39 04 15234839

#169
Nardi
Category: Jewelry
Address: Sestiere S. Marco, 71/A
30124 Venezia Italy
Phone: +39 04 15232150

#170
ON B
Category: Fashion
Address: Sestiere S. Marco, 5051
30124 Venezia Italy
Phone: +39 04 12960493

#171
Testolini
Category: Art Supplies
Address: Sestiere S. Marco, 4744
30124 Venezia Italy
Phone: +39 04 15229265

#172
Vianello / GiancArlo
Category: Flowers & Gifts
Address: Sestiere S. Marco, 67
30124 Venezia Italy
Phone: +39 04 15221387

#173
Zeta Sport
Category: Sporting Goods
Address: Sestiere S. Marco, 4526
30124 Venezia Italy
Phone: +39 04 15207272

#174
4 WIN
Category: Lingerie
Address: Sestiere S. Marco, 4672
30124 Venezia Italy
Phone: +39 04 15237412

#175
A.R.P. Advanced Retail Project
Category: Flowers & Gifts
Address: Sestiere S. Marco, 783
30124 Venezia Italy
Phone: +39 04 12412526

#176
BBB
Category: Fashion
Address: Sestiere S. Marco, 1744/48
30124 Venezia Italy
Phone: +39 04 12960321

#177
Bartolucci Italy
Category: Arts & Crafts
Address: Sestiere S. Marco, 5163
30124 Venezia Italy
Phone: +39 04 15221960

#178
B. & B. ART
di Bugno Massimiliano
Category: Art Gallery
Address: Sestiere S. Marco, 1996
30124 Venezia Italy
Phone: +39 04 15230360

#179
Biblos SNC di CArlo Docupil
Category: Cards & Stationery
Address: Sestiere S. Marco, 2087
30124 Venezia Italy
Phone: +39 04 15210714

#180
Boldrin Gioielli S.N.C.
di Carlo e Vladimiro Boldrin
Category: Jewelry
Address: Sestiere S. Marco, 62/A
30124 Venezia Italy
Phone: +39 04 15200572

#181
Bottega Dell'arte
di Scarpa Gabriele
Category: Art Supplies
Address: Sestiere S. Marco, 1758
30124 Venezia Italy
Phone: +39 04 12770812

#182
Caponsacco-De Lorenzi
Theresa Maria
Category: Flowers & Gifts
Address: Sestiere S. Marco, 4340
30124 Venezia Italy
Phone: +39 04 12413256

#183
Ferruzzi
Category: Eyewear & Opticians
Address: Sestiere S. Marco, 141
30124 Venezia Italy
Phone: +39 04 15222605

#184
Fortuny SAS di Lando Lino
Category: Arts & Crafts
Address: Sestiere S. Marco, 298
30124 Venezia Italy
Phone: +39 04 15226791

#185
Galleria Luce Arte Moderna
Category: Art Gallery
Address: Sestiere S. Marco, 1922/A
30124 Venezia Italy
Phone: +39 04 15222949

#186
Girardi / Alessandro
Category: Tobacco Shop
Address: Sestiere S. Marco, 4738
30124 Venezia Italy
Phone: +39 04 15226348

#187
Jiang Pingping
Category: Jewelry
Address: Sestiere S. Marco, 918
30124 Venezia Italy
Phone: +39 04 15236390

#188
**Luisadue SAS
di Maria Luisa Filippucci**
Category: Lingerie
Address: Sestiere S. Marco, 1693
30124 Venezia Italy
Phone: +39 04 15223020

#189
Lyra di Folin Luca
Category: Fashion
Address: Sestiere S. Marco, 714
30124 Venezia Italy
Phone: +39 04 12410879

#190
Macri' di DE Nobili Umberto
Category: Shoe Store
Address: Sestiere S. Marco, 1340
30124 Venezia Italy
Phone: +39 04 15231221

#191
MD di Miatto Daniela
Category: Flowers & Gifts
Address: Via Sestiere SAN Marco, 5380
30124 Venezia Italy
Phone: +39 04 15230204

#192
Nitta Gioielli
Category: Jewelry
Address: Sestiere S. Marco, 1298
30124 Venezia Italy
Phone: +39 04 15201048

#193
Sellier Gioielli
Category: Jewelry
Address: Sestiere S. Marco, 3708
30124 Venezia Italy
Phone: +39 04 15235202

#194
Solaris Italia
Category: Eyewear & Opticians
Address: Sestiere S. Marco, 264
30124 Venezia Italy
Phone: +39 04 12413818

#195
Stefanel
Category: Fashion
Address: Sestiere S. Marco, 729
30124 Venezia Italy
Phone: +39 04 15223838

#196
Tristar
Category: Flowers & Gifts
Address: Sestiere S. Marco, 1093
30124 Venezia Italy
Phone: +39 04 15230347

#197
Vergombello Roberto
Category: Jewelry
Address: Via SAN Marco, 1565/A
30124 Venezia Italy
Phone: +39 04 15237821

#198
Lvmh Italia
Category: Leather Goods
Address: Sestiere S. Marco, 1255
30124 Venezia Italy
Phone: +39 04 15224500

#199
Salvadori
Category: Jewelry
Address: Sestiere S. Marco, 5022
30124 Venezia Italy
Phone: +39 04 15209620

#200
Aldo Temin
Category: Leather Goods
Address: Sestiere S. Marco, 4954
30124 Venezia Italy
Phone: +39 04 15230611

#201
Araba Fenice
Category: Fashion
Address: Sestiere S. Marco, 1822
30124 Venezia Italy
Phone: +39 04 15220664

#202
Bivuelle
Category: Jewelry
Address: Sestiere S. Marco, 13
30124 Venezia Italy
Phone: +39 04 15207854

#203
Brocca Paolo
Category: Fashion
Address: Sestiere S. Marco, 4673
30124 Venezia Italy
Phone: +39 04 12770147

#204
Araba Fenice
Category: Fashion
Address: Sestiere S. Marco, 1822
30124 Venezia Italy
Phone: +39 04 15220664

#205
Bivuelle
Category: Jewelry
Address: Sestiere S. Marco, 13
30124 Venezia Italy
Phone: +39 04 15207854

#206
Brocca Paolo
Category: Fashion
Address: Sestiere S. Marco, 4673
30124 Venezia Italy
Phone: +39 04 12770147

#207
Codogno Aldo
Category: Arts & Crafts
Address: Sestiere S. Marco, 828
30124 Venezia Italy
Phone: +39 04 15287359

#208
Feda
Category: Watches
Address: Sestiere S. Marco, 257
30124 Venezia Italy
Phone: +39 04 15230613

#209
Forven
Category: Men's Clothing
Address: Sestiere S. Marco, 4928
30124 Venezia Italy
Phone: +39 04 15229020

#210
Galleria Rossella Junck
Category: Antiques
Address: Sestiere S. Marco, 2360
30124 Venezia Italy
Phone: +39 04 15207747

#211
Galleria Traghetto
Category: Art Gallery
Address: Sestiere S. Marco, 2543
30124 Venezia Italy
Phone: +39 04 15221188

#212
Giuliam
Category: Fashion
Address: Sestiere S. Marco, 1810
30124 Venezia Italy
Phone: +39 04 12410990

#213
Jeans Pull
Category: Fashion
Address: Sestiere S. Marco, 236
30124 Venezia Italy
Phone: +39 04 15230105

#214
**Sitran di Doni Ileana
e Sitran Daniela**
Category: Arts & Crafts
Address: Sestiere S. Marco, 411
30124 Venezia Italy
Phone: +39 04 15208979

#215
Simonato Bruno
Category: Jewelry
Address: Sestiere S. Marco, 148
30124 Venezia Italy
Phone: +39 04 15200772

#216
Studio Arga di Gabriella Tallon
Category: Art Gallery
Address: Sestiere S. Marco, 3659/A
30124 Venezia Italy
Phone: +39 04 12411124

#217
Veneziana Mobiliare
Category: Jewelry
Address: Sestiere S. Marco, 606
30124 Venezia Italy
Phone: +39 04 15222071

#218
Vesco / Silvano
Category: Jewelry
Address: Sestiere S. Marco, 75
30124 Venezia Italy
Phone: +39 04 15203853

#219
Antoniamiletto
Category: Jewelry
Address: Sestiere S. Marco, 3209
30124 Venezia Italy
Phone: +39 04 15205177

#220
Antiquus
Category: Antiques
Address: Sestiere S. Marco, 2973
30124 Venezia Italy
Phone: +39 04 15206395

#221
Astolfo Simonato Veronica
Category: Jewelry
Address: Sestiere S. Marco, 738
30124 Venezia Italy
Phone: +39 04 12960640

#222
B & B di Bari Paolo
Category: Jewelry
Address: Sestiere S. Marco, 346
30124 Venezia Italy
Phone: +39 04 15231861

#223
Bertoni / Alberto
Category: Bookstore
Address: Sestiere S. Marco, 3637/B
30124 Venezia Italy
Phone: +39 04 15229583

#224
Boccanegra / Rita
Category: Flowers & Gifts
Address: Sestiere S. Marco, 4371
30124 Venezia Italy
Phone: +39 04 15232113

#225
Bruno Magli
Category: Shoe Store
Address: Sestiere S. Marco, 1302
30124 Venezia Italy
Phone: +39 04 15227210

#226
Chen / Xiao Ping
Category: Leather Goods
Address: Sestiere S. Marco,
30124 Venezia Italy
Phone: +39 04 15237814

#227
DE Martin / Laura
Category: Tobacco Shop
Address: Sestiere S. Marco, 1061
30124 Venezia Italy
Phone: +39 04 12770875

#228
D.G.S.
Category: Fashion
Address: Sestiere S. Marco, 223
30124 Venezia Italy
Phone: +39 04 12777770

#229
D.G.S.
Category: Fashion
Address: Sestiere S. Marco, 957
30124 Venezia Italy
Phone: +39 04 15282282

#230
Diesel Italia
Category: Fashion
Address: Sestiere S. Marco, 5315
30124 Venezia Italy
Phone: +39 04 12413321

#231
Exclusive SAS di Franco Paola
Category: Fashion
Address: Sestiere S. Marco, 717
30124 Venezia Italy
Phone: +39 04 15205639

#232
Galleria Il Capricorno
Category: Art Gallery
Address: Sestiere San Marco 1994
30124 Venezia Italy
Phone: +39 04 15206920

#233
Garbeglio / Andrea
Category: Tobacco Shop
Address: Sestiere S. Marco, 1150
30124 Venezia Italy
Phone: +39 04 15200958

#234
Gasparini / Andreina
Category: Tobacco Shop
Address: Sestiere S. Marco, 5122
30124 Venezia Italy
Phone: +39 04 15235024

#235
Galleria Daniele Luchetta
Category: Art Gallery
Address: Sestiere San Marco 2513A
30124 Venezia Italy
Phone: +39 04 15285092

#236
Galleria D'arte Contini
Category: Art Gallery
Address: Sestiere San Marco 2765
30124 Venezia Italy
Phone: +39 04 15208381

#237
Geox
Category: Shoe Store
Address: Sestiere S. Marco, 4943
30124 Venezia Italy
Phone: +39 04 12413182

#238
L.F.A.
Category: Lingerie
Address: Sestiere S. Marco, 3537
30124 Venezia Italy
Phone: +39 04 15230578

#239
Libreria Linea D'acqua S.A.S.
di Zentilini Luca
Category: Bookstore
Address: Sestiere S. Marco, 3717/D
30124 Venezia Italy
Phone: +39 04 15224030

#240
Libreria Goldoni
Category: Bookstore
Address: Sestiere S. Marco, 4742
30124 Venezia Italy
Phone: +39 04 15222384

#241
Luxury Goods Italia
Category: Fashion
Address: Sestiere S. Marco, 1316
30124 Venezia Italy
Phone: +39 04 15230477

#242
Luxury Goods Italia
Category: Fashion
Address: Sestiere S. Marco, 2102
30124 Venezia Italy
Phone: +39 04 15200049

#243
Lvmh Italia
Category: Leather Goods
Address: Sestiere S. Marco, 1601
30124 Venezia Italy
Phone: +39 04 12415631

#244
Mavi's Pelletterie
di Bognolo Chiara
Category: Leather Goods
Address: Sestiere S. Marco, 1007/A
30124 Venezia Italy
Phone: +39 04 15203024

#245
MAX Mara
Category: Fashion
Address: Sestiere S. Marco, 5033
30124 Venezia Italy
Phone: +39 04 15226688

#246
Novello Michele
Category: Art Gallery
Address: Sestiere San Marco 2016 A
30124 Venezia Italy
Phone: +39 04 15285599

#247
Orlandini Gioielli
Category: Jewelry
Address: Sestiere S. Marco, 77
30124 Venezia Italy
Phone: +39 04 15231048

#248
Ottica Urbani Franco S.N.C.
di Lorenzo Urbani
Category: Eyewear & Opticians
Address: Sestiere S. Marco, 1280
30124 Venezia Italy
Phone: +39 04 15224140

#249
Paradiso del Bebe'
di Vianello Renata
Category: Children's Clothing
Address: Sestiere S. Marco, 678
30124 Venezia Italy
Phone: +39 04 15220914

#250
Panisson / Lorenzo
Category: Tobacco Shop
Address: Sestiere S. Marco, 113
30124 Venezia Italy
Phone: +39 04 15238161

#251
Piliego Elisabetta
Category: Cosmetics & Beauty Supply
Address: Sestiere S. Marco, 5207
30124 Venezia Italy
Phone: +39 04 15289408

#252
Promod Italia
Category: Fashion
Address: Sestiere S. Marco, 5378
30124 Venezia Italy
Phone: +39 04 12410668

#253
Reflections di Uscotti Franco
Category: Arts & Crafts
Address: Sestiere S. Marco, 946/A
30124 Venezia Italy
Phone: +39 04 15287082

#254
Shopping Center
Category: Arts & Crafts
Address: Sestiere S. Marco, 418
30124 Venezia Italy
Phone: +39 04 15200171

#255
Solaris Italia
Category: Eyewear & Opticians
Address: Sestiere S. Marco, 5044
30124 Venezia Italy
Phone: +39 04 12413794

#256
Stevens / Daniel Maguire
Category: Arts & Crafts
Address: Sestiere S. Marco, 3285/A
30124 Venezia Italy
Phone: +39 04 15227563

#257
Time Concept
Category: Watches
Address: Sestiere S. Marco, 2056
30124 Venezia Italy
Phone: +39 04 12412021

#258
Tokatzian
Category: Jewelry
Address: Sestiere S. Marco, 18
30124 Venezia Italy
Phone: +39 04 15233821

#259
Trois / Martina
Category: Fashion
Address: Sestiere S. Marco, 513
30124 Venezia Italy
Phone: +39 04 15229096

#260
Zora DA Venezia di Renier Zora
Category: Flowers & Gifts
Address: Sestiere S. Marco, 2407
30124 Venezia Italy
Phone: +39 04 12770895

#261
Le Perle
Category: Jewelry
Address: Sestiere San Marco 789
30124 Venezia Italy
Phone: +39 04 15286516

#262
AL Duca D'aosta
Category: Fashion
Address: Sestiere S. Marco, 4945
30124 Venezia Italy
Phone: +39 04 15204079

#263
ART
Category: Art Gallery
Address: Sestiere San Marco 3339
30124 Venezia Italy
Phone: +39 04 15281660

#264
Bastianello / IDA
Category: Flowers & Gifts
Address: Sestiere S. Marco, 315/B
30124 Venezia Italy
Phone: +39 04 15204580

#265
Belzebu'
Category: Fashion
Address: Sestiere S. Marco, 482
30124 Venezia Italy
Phone: +39 04 15231743

#266
Bravin Renato
Category: Jewelry
Address: Sestiere S. Marco, 119
30124 Venezia Italy
Phone: +39 04 15205977

#267
Cristal Star di Monica CArli
Category: Flowers & Gifts
Address: Sestiere S. Marco, 1017
30124 Venezia Italy
Phone: +39 04 15234968

#268
Giupponi / Roberto
Category: Jewelry
Address: Sestiere S. Marco, 4487
30124 Venezia Italy
Phone: +39 04 15235287

#269
Missiaglia
Category: Jewelry
Address: Sestiere S. Marco, 125
30124 Venezia Italy
Phone: +39 04 15224464

#270
Ortolani A.
Category: Fashion
Address: Sestiere S. Marco, 89
30124 Venezia Italy
Phone: +39 04 15225719

#271
Stella S.A.S di Lando Lino
Category: Fashion
Address: Sestiere S. Marco, 2428
30124 Venezia Italy
Phone: +39 04 15200505

#272
Venuti / Lorenzo
Category: Flowers & Gifts
Address: Sestiere S. Marco, 231
30124 Venezia Italy
Phone: +39 04 15223704

#273
Vesco / Silvano
Category: Jewelry
Address: Sestiere S. Marco, 1812
30124 Venezia Italy
Phone: +39 04 12413361

#274
Viani / Anna, ottica
Category: Eyewear & Opticians
Address: Sestiere S. Marco, 700
30124 Venezia Italy
Phone: +39 04 15231135

#275
Videomat Service
di Giove Marzia
Category: Videos & Video Game Rental
Address: Sestiere S. Marco, 5249
30124 Venezia Italy
Phone: +39 04 15212928

#276
Aldo Temin SAS
di Roberto Rosanna
Category: Leather Goods
Address: Sestiere S. Marco, 5205
30124 Venezia Italy
Phone: +39 04 15204255

#277
Baranes
Category: Jewelry
Address: Sestiere S. Marco, 1586
30124 Venezia Italy
Phone: +39 04 12412687

#278
Bulgari Italia
Category: Jewelry
Address: Sestiere S. Marco, 2281
30124 Venezia Italy
Phone: +39 04 12410553

#279
B.V. Italia
Category: Leather Goods
Address: Sestiere S. Marco, 1337
30124 Venezia Italy
Phone: +39 04 15228489

#280
Bruno Magli
Category: Shoe Store
Address: Sestiere S. Marco, 1584
30124 Venezia Italy
Phone: +39 04 15223472

#281
Cecconi Corsaro
Category: Fashion
Address: Sestiere S. Marco, 1065
30124 Venezia Italy
Phone: +39 04 15238513

#282
Cinox Group International Trade
Category: Art Gallery
Address: Sestiere San Marco 79A
30124 Venezia Italy
Phone: +39 04 12412883

#283
EMI di Francesca Cappello
Category: Leather Goods
Address: Sestiere S. Marco, 3632
30124 Venezia Italy
Phone: +39 04 15231326

#284
Euroretail CKJ
Category: Fashion
Address: Sestiere S. Marco, 4599
30124 Venezia Italy
Phone: +39 04 15202164

#285
Galluppi Giovanni
Category: Cosmetics & Beauty Supply
Address: Sestiere S. Marco, 4781
30124 Venezia Italy
Phone: +39 04 15236817

#286
Giolmarine
Category: Sporting Goods
Address: Sestiere S. Marco, 3226/B
30124 Venezia Italy
Phone: +39 04 15222207

#287
Grafica Antica
di Manlio Penso &C
Category: Art Gallery
Address: Sestiere San Marco 2089
30124 Venezia Italy
Phone: +39 04 15227199

#288
Industries
Category: Fashion
Address: Sestiere S. Marco, 4574
30124 Venezia Italy
Phone: +39 04 15228485

#289
J Retail 2
Category: Fashion
Address: Sestiere S. Marco, 1066
30124 Venezia Italy
Phone: +39 04 15227156

. #290
La Galleria
Category: Art Gallery
Address: Sestiere San Marco 2566
30124 Venezia Italy
Phone: +39 04 15207415

#291
Legatoria La Fenice SNC di Lumine Luciana e Romor Renato
Category: Cards & Stationery
Address: Sestiere S. Marco, 826
30124 Venezia Italy
Phone: +39 04 15209331

#292
Levante Veneto di Boninio DR.
Category: Cards & Stationery
Address: Sestiere S. Marco, 5469
30124 Venezia Italy
Phone: +39 04 15287403

#293
Luxury Goods Italia
Category: Fashion
Address: Sestiere S. Marco, 2101
30124 Venezia Italy
Phone: +39 04 12413961

#294
L V Venezia S.A.S.
Category: Arts & Crafts
Address: Sestiere S. Marco, 171
30124 Venezia Italy
Phone: +39 04 12412352

#295
Marina Rinaldi
Category: Fashion
Address: Sestiere S. Marco, 266
30124 Venezia Italy
Phone: +39 04 12770064

#296
Marcianum Press
Category: Bookstore
Address: Sestiere S. Marco, 337/C
30124 Venezia Italy
Phone: +39 04 15222382

#297
Morellato & Sector Store
Category: Jewelry
Address: Sestiere S. Marco, 221
30124 Venezia Italy
Phone: +39 04 12960709

#298
Only ONE
Category: Jewelry
Address: Sestiere S. Marco, 719
30124 Venezia Italy
Phone: +39 04 15286517

#299
Oreficeria SAN Salvador
Category: Jewelry
Address: Sestiere S. Marco, 4840
30124 Venezia Italy
Phone: +39 04 15235135

#300
Progetto Venezia
Category: Art Gallery
Address: Sestiere San Marco 3201
30124 Venezia Italy
Phone: +39 04 15200673

#301
Roby
Category: Fashion
Address: Sestiere S. Marco, 2410
30124 Venezia Italy
Phone: +39 04 12960555

#302
Societa' Sport And Leisure Wear Corner
Category: Fashion
Address: Sestiere S. Marco, 284
30124 Venezia Italy
Phone: +39 04 15230145

#303
Tornabuoni Arte
Category: Art Gallery
Address: Sestiere San Marco 2663
30124 Venezia Italy
Phone: +39 04 15231201

#304
Calzature Macri
Category: Shoe Store
Address: Sestiere S. Marco, 420
30124 Venezia Italy
Phone: +39 04 15229956

#305
Charta
Category: Jewelry
Address: Sestiere S. Marco, 831
30124 Venezia Italy
Phone: +39 04 15229801

#306
Codognato / Attilio
Category: Jewelry
Address: Sestiere S. Marco, 1295
30124 Venezia Italy
Phone: +39 04 15225042

#307
Commerciale S. Marco
Category: Jewelry
Address: Sestiere S. Marco, 138
30124 Venezia Italy
Phone: +39 04 15220982

#308
Della Toffola / Mauro
Category: Antiques
Address: Sestiere S. Marco, 1567
30124 Venezia Italy
Phone: +39 04 15236643

#309
Emporium di Fuga Manuela
Category: Fashion
Address: Sestiere S. Marco, 670
30124 Venezia Italy
Phone: +39 04 15235911

#310
G. BEE 1920
Category: Fashion
Address: Sestiere S. Marco, 675
30124 Venezia Italy
Phone: +39 04 15229681

#311
GIO di Lorena Pitteri
Category: Jewelry
Address: Sestiere S. Marco, 4511
30124 Venezia Italy
Phone: +39 04 12410712

#312
Grisetti / Claudia
Category: Flowers & Gifts
Address: Sestiere S. Marco, 1860
30124 Venezia Italy
Phone: +39 04 15205076

#313
I Muschieri
Category: Cosmetics & Beauty Supply
Address: Sestiere S. Marco, 1177
30124 Venezia Italy
Phone: +39 04 15228940

#314
LE ROS
Category: Arts & Crafts
Address: Sestiere S. Marco, 5324
30124 Venezia Italy
Phone: +39 04 15203693

#315
Nardi
Category: Jewelry
Address: Sestiere S. Marco, 69
30124 Venezia Italy
Phone: +39 04 15225733

#316
Ottica Carraro
Category: Eyewear & Opticians
Address: Sestiere S. Marco, 3706
30124 Venezia Italy
Phone: +39 04 15204258

#317
Pignaton Vezia IN Linassi
Category: Fashion
Address: Sestiere S. Marco, 80
30124 Venezia Italy
Phone: +39 04 15224378

#318
Prova D'artista
Category: Art Gallery
Address: Sestiere San Marco 1994B
30124 Venezia Italy
Phone: +39 04 15224812

#319
Tiozzo / Roberto
Category: Jewelry
Address: Sestiere S. Marco, 740
30124 Venezia Italy
Phone: +39 04 15221217

#320
Zorzi e Ragazzi S.N.C.
Category: Flowers & Gifts
Address: Sestiere S. Marco, 71/B
30124 Venezia Italy
Phone: +39 04 15232114

#321
Zanchi / GiancArlo
Category: Tobacco Shop
Address: Sestiere S. Marco, 3531
30124 Venezia Italy
Phone: +39 04 15224644

#322
Agreement
Category: Fashion
Address: Sestiere S. Marco, 3799
30124 Venezia Italy
Phone: +39 04 12411611

#323
Artitalia
Category: Art Gallery
Address: Sestiere San Marco 3627
30124 Venezia Italy
Phone: +39 04 15280203

#324
B.V. Italia
Category: Leather Goods
Address: Sestiere S. Marco, 1461
30124 Venezia Italy
Phone: +39 04 15205197

#325
Calzature La Parigina
Category: Shoe Store
Address: Sestiere S. Marco, 733
30124 Venezia Italy
Phone: +39 04 15231555

#326
Calzature La Parigina
Category: Shoe Store
Address: Sestiere S. Marco, 4337
30124 Venezia Italy
Phone: +39 04 15231827

#327
**Canova S.A.S.
di Busato Fabrizio**
Category: Jewelry
Address: Sestiere S. Marco, 701
30124 Venezia Italy
Phone: +39 04 15220749

#328
Chen Xiao Ping
Category: Leather Goods
Address: Sestiere S. Marco, 1643
30124 Venezia Italy
Phone: +39 04 15287940

#329
Conservatorio di Musica Benedetto Marcello
Category: Opera & Ballet, Musical
Instruments, Music Venues
Address: Sestiere San Marco 2810
30124 Venezia Italy
Phone: +39 04 15225604

#330
Foot Locker Italy
Category: Shoe Store
Address: Sestiere S. Marco, 4948
30124 Venezia Italy
Phone: +39 04 12960565

#331
Gioielleria Andrea Trevisan di Bruno Spavento
Category: Jewelry
Address: Sestiere S. Marco, 111
30124 Venezia Italy
Phone: +39 04 15204007

#332
Grows di Nicola Grillo
Category: Fashion
Address: Sestiere S. Marco, 4260/B
30124 Venezia Italy
Phone: +39 04 15238457

#333
L.A. Rialto
Category: Fashion
Address: Sestiere S. Marco, 4596
30124 Venezia Italy
Phone: +39 04 12411494

#334
LE Gioie di Bortolo di Doriana Magnana
Category: Jewelry
Address: Sestiere S. Marco, 5536
30124 Venezia Italy
Phone: +39 04 15226436

#335
Liber SNC di Lumine Alfredo
Category: Cards & Stationery
Address: Sestiere S. Marco, 739
30124 Venezia Italy
Phone: +39 04 15212908

#336
La Vetrinetta di Inchiostro Claudia
Category: Arts & Crafts
Address: Sestiere S. Marco, 1853
30124 Venezia Italy
Phone: +39 04 15289477

#337
Leon D'oro SAS
di Gastaldi Marino
Category: Jewelry
Address: Sestiere S. Marco, 5330
30124 Venezia Italy
Phone: +39 04 15220626

#338
LT3
Category: Bookstore
Address: Sestiere S. Marco, 1345
30124 Venezia Italy
Phone: +39 04 15222193

#339
MAX & CO.
Category: Fashion
Address: Sestiere S. Marco, 5028
30124 Venezia Italy
Phone: +39 04 15230817

#340
Meneghetti S.A.S. di Lombardi
Marino e Meneghetti Liliana &C
Category: Jewelry
Address: Sestiere S. Marco, 5173
30124 Venezia Italy
Phone: +39 04 15237683

#341
Ottica Sapori S.A.S.
di Sapori Raffaella
Category: Eyewear & Opticians
Address: Sestiere S. Marco, 319/A
30124 Venezia Italy
Phone: +39 04 15230010

#342
Pozzato Daniela
Category: Arts & Crafts
Address: Sestiere S. Marco, 308/C
30124 Venezia Italy
Phone: +39 04 15239344

#343
Quel CHE Manca
Category: Antiques
Address: Sestiere S. Marco, 3965
30124 Venezia Italy
Phone: +39 04 15222681

#344
Ro.Ro.
Category: Leather Goods
Address: Sestiere S. Marco, 4833
30124 Venezia Italy
Phone: +39 04 12770460

#345
Rossetti F.lli
Category: Shoe Store
Address: Sestiere S. Marco, 4800
30124 Venezia Italy
Phone: +39 04 15230571

#346
Rocca
Category: Fashion
Address: Sestiere S. Marco, 1494
30124 Venezia Italy
Phone: +39 04 12770661

#347
Salvatore Ferragamo Italia
Category: Shoe Store
Address: Sestiere S. Marco, 2098
30124 Venezia Italy
Phone: +39 04 12778509

#348
Sartori Simonetta
Category: Fashion
Address: Sestiere S. Marco, 4455
30124 Venezia Italy
Phone: +39 04 12776380

#349
Segreti Veneziani
di Belardinelli Matteo
Category: Jewelry
Address: Sestiere S. Marco, 5335
30124 Venezia Italy
Phone: +39 04 15238483

#350
Zeta
Category: Leather Goods
Address: Sestiere S. Marco, 1104
30124 Venezia Italy
Phone: +39 04 15280097

#351
Vorano / Giovanni
Category: Arts & Crafts
Address: Sestiere S. Marco, 1492
30124 Venezia Italy
Phone: +39 04 15221329

#352
**Zecchi Calzature
di Visnadi Annamaria**
Category: Shoe Store
Address: Sestiere S. Marco, 213
30124 Venezia Italy
Phone: +39 04 15232090

#353
**Antichita' SAN Samuele
di Silvana Vianello**
Category: Antiques
Address: Sestiere S. Marco, 3130
30124 Venezia Italy
Phone: +39 04 15204900

#354
Bally Italia
Category: Shoe Store
Address: Sestiere S. Marco, 4919
30124 Venezia Italy
Phone: +39 04 15285839

#355
Bettinello - Gioielleria
Category: Jewelry
Address: Sestiere S. Marco, 4154
30124 Venezia Italy
Phone: +39 04 15224490

#356
Black Watch TWO
Category: Men's Clothing
Address: Sestiere S. Marco, 4594/A
30124 Venezia Italy
Phone: +39 04 15231945

#357
Bertoni / Alberto
Category: Bookstore
Address: Sestiere S. Marco, 4718
30124 Venezia Italy
Phone: +39 04 15224615

#358
**Boldrin S.N.C.
di Vladimiro e Carlo Boldrin**
Category: Jewelry
Address: Sestiere S. Marco, 64
30124 Venezia Italy
Phone: +39 04 15223197

#359
Bona
Category: Leather Goods
Address: Sestiere S. Marco, 5021
30124 Venezia Italy
Phone: +39 04 15225763

#360
Dittura / Gianni
Category: Shoe Store
Address: Sestiere S. Marco, 943
30124 Venezia Italy
Phone: +39 04 15223502

#361
Doge di Campaner Annalisa
Category: Jewelry
Address: Sestiere S. Marco, 928
30124 Venezia Italy
Phone: +39 04 15237494

#362
Elena
Category: Jewelry
Address: Sestiere S. Marco, 215/216
30124 Venezia Italy
Phone: +39 04 15226540

#363
Ella Baby
Category: Children's Clothing
Address: Sestiere S. Marco, 4471/A
30124 Venezia Italy
Phone: +39 04 15236688

#364
Ferruzzi
Category: Eyewear & Opticians
Address: Sestiere S. Marco, 709
30124 Venezia Italy
Phone: +39 04 15223098

#365
**Gioielleria Carraro
di Carraro Pierpaolo**
Category: Jewelry
Address: Sestiere S. Marco, 4816
30124 Venezia Italy
Phone: +39 04 15286988

#366
Gruppo Coin
Category: Shopping Center, Grocery
Address: Sestiere S. Marco, 4546
30124 Venezia Italy
Phone: +39 04 15238444

#367
Lumine / Marina
Category: Tobacco Shop
Address: Sestiere S. Marco, 481
30124 Venezia Italy
Phone: +39 04 15238852

#368
Mazzucchi
Category: Art Gallery
Address: Sestiere San Marco 1771
30124 Venezia Italy
Phone: +39 04 15207045

#369
Minotto / Luigi
Category: Jewelry
Address: Sestiere S. Marco, 4876
30124 Venezia Italy
Phone: +39 04 15222256

#370
Minotto / Luigi
Category: Jewelry
Address: Sestiere S. Marco, 4464
30124 Venezia Italy
Phone: +39 04 15231197

#371
ONS
Category: Fashion
Address: Sestiere S. Marco, 1341
30124 Venezia Italy
Phone: +39 04 15204386

#372
Roby
Category: Fashion
Address: Sestiere S. Marco, 1673
30124 Venezia Italy
Phone: +39 04 15231273

#373
Sartori / Renata
Category: Shoe Store
Address: Sestiere S. Marco, 1699
30124 Venezia Italy
Phone: +39 04 15222795

#374
THE Disney Store Italia
Category: Toy Store
Address: Sestiere S. Marco, 5257
30124 Venezia Italy
Phone: +39 04 15223980

#375
Toso / Luciano
Category: Tobacco Shop
Address: Sestiere S. Marco, 3634
30124 Venezia Italy
Phone: +39 04 15230283

#376
Vesco & Sambo
Category: Jewelry
Address: Sestiere San Marco 102
30124 Venezia Italy
Phone: +39 04 15223347

#377
Venice Design
Category: Art Gallery
Address: Sestiere San Marco 1310
30124 Venezia Italy
Phone: +39 04 15238530

#378
Zanetti
Category: Fashion
Address: Sestiere S. Marco, 670
30124 Venezia Italy
Phone: +39 04 15229992

#379
Zinato Maria Luisa
Category: Antiques
Address: Sestiere S. Marco, 584
30124 Venezia Italy
Phone: +39 04 15231412

#380
Alien UNO
Category: Fashion
Address: Sestiere SAN Marco, 1475
30124 Venezia Italy
Phone: +39 04 12777893

#381
Alien DUE S.A.S.
di Stefano Boni
Category: Fashion
Address: Sestiere S. Marco, 1814
30124 Venezia Italy
Phone: +39 04 15205733

#382
Al.max Gallery S.N.C.
di Magro Alberto
Category: Tobacco Shop
Address: Sestiere S. Marco, 5317
30124 Venezia Italy
Phone: +39 04 15236372

#383
Arnaboldi
Category: Fashion
Address: Sestiere S. Marco, 1349/50
30124 Venezia Italy
Phone: +39 04 15221785

#384
Arte Ve.d.o.
Category: Eyewear & Opticians
Address: Sestiere S. Marco, 2436
30124 Venezia Italy
Phone: +39 04 12960765

#385
B. & B. Art
di Bugno Massimiliano
Category: Art Gallery
Address: Sestiere San Marco 1654
30124 Venezia Italy
Phone: +39 04 15288135

#386
Boutique MArly's
Category: Fashion
Address: Sestiere S. Marco, 1321
30124 Venezia Italy
Phone: +39 04 15223851

#387
Calzaturificio Donna Carolina
Category: Art Gallery
Address: Sestiere San Marco 1491
30124 Venezia Italy
Phone: +39 04 15225034

#388
Calzature La Parigina
Category: Shoe Store
Address: Sestiere S. Marco, 727/B
30124 Venezia Italy
Phone: +39 04 15226743

#389
Casella di Giuseppe
e Giovanni Scarpa
Category: Shoe Store
Address: Sestiere S. Marco, 5048
30124 Venezia Italy
Phone: +39 04 15228848

#390
Chopard Italia
Category: Jewelry
Address: Sestiere S. Marco, 51
30124 Venezia Italy
Phone: +39 04 15231883

#391
Effegi Gallery di Vianello Luciana
Category: Arts & Crafts
Address: Sestiere S. Marco, 4578/B
30124 Venezia Italy
Phone: +39 04 17241075

#392
Elysee di Rinaldini Andrea
Category: Fashion
Address: Sestiere S. Marco, 4485/A
30124 Venezia Italy
Phone: +39 04 15236948

#393
Fendi Shop
Category: Leather Goods
Address: Sestiere S. Marco, 1474
30124 Venezia Italy
Phone: +39 04 12778532

#394
Fortuny SAS di Lando Lino
Category: Fashion
Address: Sestiere S. Marco, 4753
30124 Venezia Italy
Phone: +39 04 15283537

#395
Galleria D'arte Moderna Ravagnan
di L. Ravagnan
Category: Art Gallery
Address: Sestiere San Marco 50A
30124 Venezia Italy
Phone: +39 04 15230751

#396
Gastaldi Flavio
Category: Jewelry
Address: Sestiere S. Marco, 283
30124 Venezia Italy
Phone: +39 04 15237534

#397
Giuliano Costantino
Category: Jewelry
Address: Sestiere S. Marco, 1007
30124 Venezia Italy
Phone: +39 04 15231622

#398
**Incanto Veneziano
di Palmarini Stefano**
Category: Arts & Crafts
Address: Sestiere S. Marco, 922
30124 Venezia Italy
Phone: +39 04 15229702

#399
Jade Martine & Company
Category: Lingerie
Address: Sestiere S. Marco, 1645
30124 Venezia Italy
Phone: +39 04 15212892

#400
Kiton
Category: Men's Clothing
Address: Sestiere S. Marco, 1261
30124 Venezia Italy
Phone: +39 04 12413049

#401
Kleine Galerie di Gorini Federico
Category: Art Gallery
Address: Sestiere San Marco
30124 Venezia Italy
Phone: +39 04 15222177

#402
Jeans Pull
Category: Sporting Goods
Address: Sestiere S. Marco, 4663
30124 Venezia Italy
Phone: +39 04 15225260

#403
Jeans Pull di Carretta Gianfranco
Category: Sporting Goods
Address: Sestiere S. Marco, 4715
30124 Venezia Italy
Phone: +39 04 12410703

#404
La Corniola di Marzi Gino
Category: Jewelry
Address: Sestiere S. Marco, 346
30124 Venezia Italy
Phone: +39 04 15229411

#405
Juris & Perl
Category: Art Gallery
Address: Sestiere San Marco 2950
30124 Venezia Italy
Phone: +39 04 15220603

#406
Leale Abbigliamento
Category: Fashion
Address: Sestiere S. Marco, 4462
30124 Venezia Italy
Phone: +39 04 15226292

#407
**Mavi S.N.C. di Morellato Sara
e Michielon Sebastiano**
Category: Fashion
Address: Sestiere S. Marco, 4459
30124 Venezia Italy
Phone: +39 04 15221414

#408
**Milliaccio di Chiara
& CArlo Ravagnan**
Category: Shoe Store
Address: Sestiere S. Marco, 686
30124 Venezia Italy
Phone: +39 04 15225322

#409
Ottica Mantovani
Category: Eyewear & Opticians
Address: Sestiere S. Marco, 4860
30124 Venezia Italy
Phone: +39 04 15223427

#410
**Padoan Lorenzo
& Cecconi Riccardo**
Category: Fashion
Address: Sestiere S. Marco, 660
30124 Venezia Italy
Phone: +39 04 15223892

#411
**Padoan Lorenzo
e Cecconi Riccardo**
Category: Fashion
Address: Sestiere S. Marco, 659/64
30124 Venezia Italy
Phone: +39 04 15212731

#412
**Raffaella S.N.C.
di Stefano Spagnol**
Category: Leather Goods
Address: Sestiere S. Marco, 5323
30124 Venezia Italy
Phone: +39 04 15238551

#413
Roby
Category: Fashion
Address: Sestiere S. Marco, 2030
30124 Venezia Italy
Phone: +39 04 17241022

#414
Roby
Category: Fashion
Address: Sestiere S. Marco, 2366
30124 Venezia Italy
Phone: +39 04 15224299

#415
Salvadori
Category: Jewelry
Address: Sestiere S. Marco, 4993
30124 Venezia Italy
Phone: +39 04 15228706

#416
**Shout S.N.C. di Dalla Costa
F. e Senigaglia E.**
Category: Fashion
Address: Sestiere SAN Marco, 5417
30124 Venezia Italy
Phone: +39 04 15224318

#417
**Tabaccheria N.13
di Luciani Massimiliano**
Category: Tobacco Shop
Address: Sestiere S. Marco, 5369
30124 Venezia Italy
Phone: +39 04 12411437

#418
Venice Design
Category: Art Gallery
Address: Sestiere San Marco 3146
30124 Venezia Italy
Phone: +39 04 15207915

#419
Zhang / Deguang
Category: Leather Goods
Address: Sestiere S. Marco, 846
30124 Venezia Italy
Phone: +39 04 12770202

#420
Convento Marisa
Category: Jewelry
Address: Calle DE La Mandola, 3805
30124 Venezia Italy
Phone: +39 04 15230292

#421
Alien UNO
Category: Fashion
Address: Via SAN Marco, 1475
30124 Venezia Italy
Phone: +39 04 12777893

#422
**Luna Creazione
di Annabella Daros**
Category: Antiques
Address: Via SAN Marco, 1850
30100 Venezia Italy
Phone: +39 04 15238006

#423
Perth di Fadalti Monica
Category: Shoe Store
Address: Via SAN Marco, 711
30124 Venezia Italy
Phone: +39 04 15210536

#424
Bijoumanie
Category: Jewelry
Address: Via SAN Marco, 1806
30124 Venezia Italy
Phone: +39 04 15209467

#425
DA Mosto ADA / ADA
Category: Antiques
Address: Via SAN Marco, 1812/A
30124 Venezia Italy
Phone: +39 04 15288208

#426
La Frangia SRL Il Papiro
Category: Flowers & Gifts
Address: Via SAN Marco, 2764
30124 Venezia Italy
Phone: +39 04 15223055

#427
Paropamiso S.N.C.
di Paciello Michel
Category: Oriental Goods
Address: Via SAN Marco, 1701
30124 Venezia Italy
Phone: +39 04 15227120

#428
Antichita' Mirate
di Francesco Saverio
Category: Antiques
Address: Via SAN Marco, 1904
30124 Venezia Italy
Phone: +39 04 15227600

#429
Bastianello Arte
Category: Jewelry
Address: Via SAN Marco, 5041
30124 Venezia Italy
Phone: +39 04 15226751

#430
Bottega Della Pipa
di Lanza Elisabetta
Category: Tobacco Shop
Address: Via SAN Marco, 4812
30124 Venezia Italy
Phone: +39 04 15224164

#431
Gianolla Claudio
Category: Antiques
Address: Via SAN Marco, 2766
30124 Venezia Italy
Phone: +39 04 15212652

#432
Girotto Melita e Cappellotto P e
Category: Flowers & Gifts
Address: Via SAN Marco, 1254/D
30124 Venezia Italy
Phone: +39 04 15237322

#433
La Frangia SRL Il Papiro
Category: Flowers & Gifts
Address: Via SAN Marco, 5463
30124 Venezia Italy
Phone: +39 04 12411466

#434
Barbalich
Category: Fashion
Address: Via SAN Marco, 4800
30124 Venezia Italy
Phone: +39 04 15228183

#435
Il Giullare
Category: Arts & Crafts
Address: Via Canareggio, 4293
30125 Venezia Italy
Phone: +39 04 12412369

#436
Tosatto
Category: Jewelry
Address: Via S. Polo, 73
30125 Venezia Italy
Phone: +39 04 15204088

#437
Urbani Diego Creazioni Orafe
Category: Jewelry
Address: Via S.polo, 257/A
30125 Venezia Italy
Phone: +39 04 15221108

#438
Dolce / Massimiliano
Category: Arts & Crafts
Address: Sestiere Dorsoduro, 1057/A
30123 Venezia Italy
Phone: +39 04 15220941

#439
Grant S.A.S. di Rocca Antonio
Category: Fashion
Address: Sestiere Dorsoduro, 1057/E
30123 Venezia Italy
Phone: +39 04 15227727

#440
Il Baule BLU
Category: Antiques
Address: Via S. Polo, 2916/A
30125 Venezia Italy
Phone: +39 04 1719448

#441
Seno Francesca Articoli Veneziani
Category: Arts & Crafts
Address: Via S. Polo, 2118
30125 Venezia Italy
Phone: +39 04 1720862

#442
Andreatta Sport
Category: Fashion
Address: Via Cannaregio, 4394
30121 Venezia Italy
Phone: +39 04 15230719

#443
**Profumeria Mila
di Paola Zanutto / Paola**
Category: Cosmetics & Beauty Supply
Address: Via Cannaregio, 1645/46
30121 Venezia Italy
Phone: +39 04 1717890

#444
Trimar Elettronica SRL / Nicola
Category: Sporting Goods
Address: Via Cannaregio, 1536/A
30124 Venezia Italy
Phone: +39 04 1405061

#445
Poggi Andrea / Andrea
Category: Tobacco Shop
Address: Via Cannareggio, 4616
30121 Venezia Italy
Phone: +39 04 15231636

#446
A.S.F. + Piazza
Category: Sporting Goods
Address: Sestiere SAN Polo, 13
30125 Venezia Italy
Phone: +39 04 15225638

#447
IN Auge
Category: Fashion
Address: Sestiere SAN Polo, 1067
30125 Venezia Italy
Phone: +39 04 15206547

#448
Intimo Antonella
Category: Lingerie
Address: Sestiere SAN Polo, 1052
30125 Venezia Italy
Phone: +39 04 15209925

#449
Mazzoni / Marina
Category: Children's Clothing
Address: Sestiere SAN Polo, 475
30125 Venezia Italy
Phone: +39 04 15287650

#450
Calzature Baldan Andrea
Category: Shoe Store
Address: Via Sestiere SAN Polo, 3047
30125 Venezia Italy
Phone: +39 04 15287501

#451
Calzature Parutto
Category: Shoe Store
Address: Sestiere SAN Polo, 696
30125 Venezia Italy
Phone: +39 04 15231455

#452
**Fabbro / Angelo,
Calzature e Pantofole**
Category: Shoe Store
Address: Sestiere SAN Polo, 97
30125 Venezia Italy
Phone: +39 04 15239833

#453
Il Pavone di Pelosin Paolo
Category: Cards & Stationery
Address: Sestiere SAN Polo, 1478
30125 Venezia Italy
Phone: +39 04 15224296

#454
Mizar
Category: Toy Store
Address: Sestiere SAN Polo, 383/386
30125 Venezia Italy
Phone: +39 04 12411503

#455
**Profumeria Adry
di Scarpa Adriana**
Category: Cosmetics & Beauty Supply
Address: Sestiere SAN Polo, 1576
30125 Venezia Italy
Phone: +39 04 15241249

#456
Segreti Veneziani
di Belardinelli Matteo
Category: Jewelry
Address: Sestiere SAN Polo, 79
30125 Venezia Italy
Phone: +39 04 15220647

#457
La Corte dei Miracoli
di Scintu Annamaria
Category: Arts & Crafts
Address: Sestiere SAN Polo, 1862
30125 Venezia Italy
Phone: +39 04 15221500

#458
Cimarosto / Ileana
Category: Jewelry
Address: Sestiere SAN Polo, 29
30125 Venezia Italy
Phone: +39 04 15238171

#459
Diana
Category: Flowers & Gifts
Address: Sestiere SAN Polo, 78
30125 Venezia Italy
Phone: +39 04 15229599

#460
Invernici / Luigia
Category: Fashion
Address: Sestiere SAN Polo, 1075
30125 Venezia Italy
Phone: +39 04 15227859

#461
L Angolo D ORO
Category: Jewelry
Address: Sestiere SAN Polo, 2543
30125 Venezia Italy
Phone: +39 04 15237166

#462
Maglieria Miriam
Category: Fashion
Address: Sestiere SAN Polo, 408
30125 Venezia Italy
Phone: +39 04 15228899

#463
Miba ART di Barozzi Emma
Category: Flowers & Gifts
Address: Sestiere SAN Polo, 1589
30125 Venezia Italy
Phone: +39 04 15244395

#464
Portolano / Patrizia
Category: Leather Goods
Address: Sestiere SAN Polo, 1077
30125 Venezia Italy
Phone: +39 04 15226671

#465
Zanon / Ines
Category: Cosmetics & Beauty Supply
Address: Sestiere SAN Polo, 696/A
30125 Venezia Italy
Phone: +39 04 15200232

#466
Calzature Parutto
Category: Shoe Store
Address: Sestiere SAN Polo, 786
30125 Venezia Italy
Phone: +39 04 12411453

#467
Centro Estetico La Rosa S.A.S.
Category: Cosmetics & Beauty Supply
Address: Sestiere SAN Polo, 1279
30125 Venezia Italy
Phone: +39 04 15282329

#468
Cheaply Spaccio Moda
Category: Fashion
Address: Sestiere SAN Polo, 2900/A
30125 Venezia Italy
Phone: +39 04 15245351

#469
Facco / Davide
Category: Tobacco Shop
Address: Sestiere SAN Polo, 2424
30125 Venezia Italy
Phone: +39 04 15240305

#470
HU Kedeng
Category: Leather Goods
Address: Via Sestiere SAN Polo, 33
30125 Venezia Italy
Phone: +39 04 15233319

#471
Melori & Rosenberg
Category: Art Gallery
Address: Sestiere Di San Polo 2815
30125 Venezia Italy
Phone: +39 04 12750025

#472
Pelletterie Natali
Category: Leather Goods
Address: Sestiere SAN Polo,
30125 Venezia Italy
Phone: +39 04 15208932

#473
Parutto Riccardo
Category: Shoe Store
Address: Sestiere SAN Polo, 781
30125 Venezia Italy
Phone: +39 04 15237740

#474
Queen OF Casablanca
Category: Fashion
Address: Sestiere SAN Polo, 773
30125 Venezia Italy
Phone: +39 04 15223917

#475
Seel
Category: Fashion
Address: Sestiere SAN Polo, 233
30125 Venezia Italy
Phone: +39 04 15208669

#476
Boscolo Gioie di Raffaella
Boscolo & C
Category: Jewelry
Address: Sestiere SAN Polo, 7
30125 Venezia Italy
Phone: +39 04 15228393

#477
Brusegan / Gianna
Category: Leather Goods
Address: Sestiere SAN Polo, 972
30125 Venezia Italy
Phone: +39 04 15236301

#478
La Bottega dei Mascareri
Category: Arts & Crafts
Address: Sestiere SAN Polo, 2720
30125 Venezia Italy
Phone: +39 04 15242887

#479
Piaroa
Category: Leather Goods
Address: Sestiere SAN Polo, 1247
30125 Venezia Italy
Phone: +39 04 15202198

#480
Sonnenblume
Category: Shoe Store
Address: Sestiere SAN Polo, 60
30125 Venezia Italy
Phone: +39 04 15285513

#481
SAN Polo Vetro di Toso Viviana
Category: Arts & Crafts
Address: Sestiere SAN Polo, 2309
30125 Venezia Italy
Phone: +39 04 1714688

#482
Il Teatro Delle Maschere
Category: Arts & Crafts
Address: Sestiere SAN Polo, 1564
30125 Venezia Italy
Phone: +39 04 12759205

#483
Fate e Folletti Al Frari di Francescon Martina
Category: Children's Clothing
Address: Sestiere SAN Polo, 3006
30125 Venezia Italy
Phone: +39 04 15228336

#484
La Corte dei Miracoli
di Scintu Annamaria
Category: Flowers & Gifts
Address: Sestiere SAN Polo, 1861/A
30125 Venezia Italy
Phone: +39 04 15244297

#485
Ottica Vascellari
di Roberto Vascellari e
Category: Eyewear & Opticians
Address: Sestiere SAN Polo, 1030
30125 Venezia Italy
Phone: +39 04 15229388

#486
Profumeria Ideal
Category: Cosmetics & Beauty Supply
Address: Sestiere SAN Polo, 2097
30125 Venezia Italy
Phone: +39 04 15223206

#487
Tiko' S.A.S. di Petretto Mirko
Category: Fashion
Address: Sestiere SAN Polo, 28
30125 Venezia Italy
Phone: +39 04 15237407

#488
Tosi Cristian
Category: Tobacco Shop
Address: Sestiere SAN Polo, 2873/A
30125 Venezia Italy
Phone: +39 04 15241756

#489
Luca / Gianni
Category: Tobacco Shop
Address: Sestiere SAN Polo, 2286
30125 Venezia Italy
Phone: +39 04 1713474

#490
Cecchi
Category: Jewelry
Address: Sestiere SAN Polo, 9
30125 Venezia Italy
Phone: +39 04 12410656

#491
**GLI Amici di Pierrot
di Ravagnan Giovanna**
Category: Flowers & Gifts
Address: Sestiere SAN Polo, 1033
30125 Venezia Italy
Phone: +39 04 15236655

#492
Nube / Franco
Category: Watches
Address: Sestiere SAN Polo, 785
30125 Venezia Italy
Phone: +39 04 15238232

#493
Barotti / Lorena
Category: Tobacco Shop
Address: Sestiere SAN Polo, 1136
30125 Venezia Italy
Phone: +39 04 15210791

#494
**V.A.V. Vence Arte Venezia
di Fornasier Giovanni**
Category: Art Gallery
Address: Sestiere SAN Polo,
30125 Venezia Italy
Phone: +39 04 15231108

#495
Calzature Baldan Roberto
Category: Shoe Store
Address: Sestiere SAN Polo, 3077
30125 Venezia Italy
Phone: +39 04 1718256

#496
Cuman / Maurizio
Category: Fashion
Address: Sestiere SAN Polo, 1572
30125 Venezia Italy
Phone: +39 04 1721767

#497
Zazu' di Federica Zamboni & C.
Category: Fashion
Address: Sestiere SAN Polo, 2750
30125 Venezia Italy
Phone: +39 04 1715426

#498
Seel
Category: Fashion
Address: Sestiere SAN Polo, 782
30125 Venezia Italy
Phone: +39 04 15289172

#499
**F.lli Lombardi di Riccardo
e Matteo Lombardi**
Category: Jewelry
Address: Sestiere SAN Polo, 2100
30125 Venezia Italy
Phone: +39 04 15232470

#500
**Frollo Gioiellerie
di Giorgio Frollo**
Category: Jewelry
Address: Sestiere SAN Polo, 2
30125 Venezia Italy
Phone: +39 04 15228756

TOP 500 RESTAURANTS

The Most Recommended by Locals & Trevelers

(From #1 to #500)

#1
La Zucca
Cuisines: Italian
Address: Sestiere Santa Croce 1762
30135 Venezia Italy
Phone: +39 04 15241570

#2
**Osteria Alla Staffa
di Berton Franco**
Cuisines: Italian
Address: Calle Del Ospedaleto 6397A
30121 Venezia Italy
Phone: +39 04 15239160

#3
Alfredo's
Cuisines: Fast Food
Address: Calle de La Casseleria 5324
30122 Venezia Italy
Phone: +39 335 5487020

#4
Cantinone Già Schiavi
Cuisines: Beer, Wine & Spirits, Italian
Address: Dorsoduro 992
30123 Venezia Italy
Phone: +39 04 15230034

#5
Da Raffaele
Cuisines: Venetian
Address: San Marco 2347
30124 Venezia Italy
Phone: +39 04 15232317

#6
Osteria alle Testiere
Cuisines: Italian
Address: Via Castello 5801
30122 Venezia Italy
Phone: +39 04 15227220

#7
Da Mamo
Cuisines: Italian, Pizza
Address: San Marco 5251
30124 Venezia Italy
Phone: +39 04 15236583

#8
Algiubagio
Cuisines: Italian
Address: Fundamente Nuove
Cannareggio 5039
30125 Venezia Italy
Phone: +39 04 15236084

#9
Antico Forno
Cuisines: Pizza, Sandwiches
Address: Via San Polo 970
30125 Venezia Italy
Phone: +39 04 15204110

#10
La Feluca
Cuisines: Italian
Address: San Marco 3648
30124 Venezia Italy
Phone: +39 412 412785

#11
Pizzeria Al Faro
Cuisines: Pizza, Italian
Address: Campo Ghetto Vecchio 1181
30121 Venezia Italy
Phone: +39 444 12750794

#12
Trattoria alla Rivetta
Cuisines: Seafood, Italian
Address: Castello 4625
30122 Venezia Italy
Phone: +39 04 15287302

#13
Rossopomodoro
Cuisines: Napoletana, Pizza
Address: Calle larga San Marco 403
30124 Venezia Italy
Phone: +39 04 12438949

#14
Trattoria Corte Sconta
Cuisines: Italian, Seafood
Address: Sestiere Castello 3886
30122 Venezia Italy
Phone: +39 04 15227024

#15
Il Caffè
Cuisines: Italian
Address: Campo Santa Margherita 2963
30174 Venezia Italy
Phone: +39 04 15287998

#16
Riviera
Cuisines: Italian
Address: Sestiere Dorsoduro 1473
30123 Venezia Italy
Phone: +39 04 15227621

#17
Osteria Enoteca San Marco
Cuisines: Italian
Address: Frezzeria San Marco1610
30124 Venezia Italy
Phone: +39 04 15285242

#18
Ai Barbacani
Cuisines: Italian
Address: Calle del Paradiso 5746
30122 Venezia Italy
Phone: +39 04 15210234

#19
Caffè Florian
Cuisines: Cafe
Address: Piazza San Marco 120
30124 Venezia Italy
Phone: +39 04 15205641

#20
La Bitta
Cuisines: Italian
Address: Calle Lunga San Barnaba 2753ª
30123 Venezia Italy
Phone: +39 04 15230531

#21
Al Timon
Cuisines: Bar, Italian
Address: Fondamenta degli Ormesini 2754
30121 Venezia Italy
Phone: +39 393 463209978

#22
Taverna San Trovaso
Cuisines: Italian
Address: Veneezia Dorsoduro 1016
30123 Venezia Italy
Phone: +39 04 15203703

#23
Pizza AL Volo
Cuisines: Pizza, Italian
Address: Via Sestiere Dorsoduro 2944
30100 Venezia Italy
Phone: +39 04 15225430

#24
Birraria La Corte
Cuisines: Italian
Address: Campo San Polo
30125 Venezia Italy
Phone: +39 04 12750570

#25
Trattoria Antica Sacrestia
Cuisines: Italian
Address: Calle della Sacrestia 4442
30122 Venezia Italy
Phone: +39 04 15230749

#26
Osteria Ai 40 Ladroni
Cuisines: Venetian
Address: Fondamenta della Sensa 3253
30121 Venezia Italy
Phone: +39 04 1715736

#27
Antiche Carampane
Cuisines: Italian
Address: San Polo 1911
30125 Venezia Italy
Phone: +39 04 15240165

#28
Osteria Al Mascaron
Cuisines: Seafood, Italian, Bistro
Address: Castello, 5225
30122 Venezia Italy
Phone: +39 04 15225995

#29
Vino Vino
Cuisines: Italian, Bar
Address: Ponte Delle Veste 2007A
30124 Venezia Italy
Phone: +39 04 12417688

#30
Al Nono Risorto
Cuisines: Venetian
Address: Sestiere S. Croce, 2337
30135 Venezia Italy
Phone: +39 04 15241169

#31
Birreria Forst
Cuisines: Sandwiches, Pub
Address: Calle delle Rasse 4540
30122 Venezia Italy
Phone: +39 04 15230557

#32
Ristorarte
Cuisines: Italian
Address: Campiello DE La Pescheria, 4
30141 Venezia Italy
Phone: +39 04 15274957

#33
Pizzeria AL Casin dei Nobili
Cuisines: Italian
Address: Sestiere Dorsoduro 2765
30123 Venezia Italy
Phone: +39 04 12411841

#34
pizzeria alla Strega
Cuisines: Italian
Address: Castello 6418
30122 Venezia Italy
Phone: +39 04 15286497

#35
Rosticceria Gislon
Cuisines: Italian
Address: San Marco 5424
30124 Venezia Italy
Phone: +39 04 15223569

#36
Osteria Bancogiro
Cuisines: Venetian
Address: San polo 122
30125 Venezia Italy
Phone: +39 04 15232061

#37
Trattoria Ca D'Oro
Cuisines: Italian
Address: Cannaregio 3912
30121 Venezia Italy
Phone: +39 04 15285324

#38
La Caravella
Cuisines: Italian
Address: Calle Larga XXII Marzo 2393
30124 Venezia Italy
Phone: +39 04 15208901

#39
All'Amarone Vineria
Cuisines: Bistro, Wine Bar
Address: Calle dei Sbianchesini
30125 Venezia Italy
Phone: +39 04 15231184

#40
Osteria da Alberto
Cuisines: Bistro
Address: Sestiere Castello 3183
30122 Venezia Italy
Phone: +39 04 15285916

#41
Osteria Enoteca Al Artisti
Cuisines: Italian
Address: Sestiere Dorsoduro 1169A
30123 Venezia Italy
Phone: +39 04 15238944

#42
Anice Stellato
Cuisines: Italian
Address: Fondamenta della Sensa 3272
30121 Venezia Italy
Phone: +39 04 1720744

#43
Lineadombra
Cuisines: Italian
Address: Dursoduro 19
30123 Venezia Italy
Phone: +39 04 12411881

#44
Antica Carbonera
Cuisines: Italian, Seafood
Address: Calle Bembo 4648
30124 Venezia Italy
Phone: +39 04 15225479

#45
Ostaria Da Rioba
Cuisines: Bistro
Address: Via Cannaregio 2552
30121 Venezia Italy
Phone: +39 04 15244379

#46
La Rosa Rossa
Cuisines: Pizza, Venetian
Address: Sestiere San Marco 3709
30124 Venezia Italy
Phone: +39 04 15234605

#47
Osteria Oliva Nera
Cuisines: Italian
Address: Castello 3417
30122 Venezia Italy
Phone: +39 04 15222170

#48
Antica Locanda Montin
Cuisines: Venetian
Address: Sestiere Dorsoduro 1147
30123 Venezia Italy
Phone: +39 04 15227151

#49
Pizzeria da Sandro
Cuisines: Bar, Pizza
Address: Via San Polo 1473
30125 Venezia Italy
Phone: +39 04 15234894

#50
Vini da Gigio
Cuisines: Italian, Bistro, European
Address: Sestiere Cannaregio 3628A
30131 Venezia Italy
Phone: +39 04 15285140

#51
Terrazza Sommariva
Cuisines: Italian
Address: Rialto-Riva del Vin 731
30125 Venezia Italy
Phone: +39 04 15231164

#52
Osteria alla Frasca
Cuisines: Seafood
Address: Corte Carità 5176
30121 Venezia Italy
Phone: +39 04 15285433

#53
Osteria L'Orto dei Mori
Cuisines: Italian
Address: Campo dei Mori 3386
30121 Venezia Italy
Phone: +39 04 15243677

#54
Al Vaporetto
Cuisines: Italian
Address: Calle Della Mandola 3726
30124 Venezia Italy
Phone: +39 04 15229498

#55
Antica Besseta
Cuisines: Italian
Address: Salizzada de Ca' Zusto
30135 Venezia Italy
Phone: +39 04 1721687

#56
Trattoria Marciana
Cuisines: Italian
Address: Santa Croce 751A
30121 Venezia Italy
Phone: +39 04 12750948

#57
San Provolo
Cuisines: Italian
Address: Campo San Provolo 4713
30122 Venezia Italy
Phone: +39 04 15285085

#58
Al Covo
Cuisines: Italian
Address: Via Castello 3968
30122 Venezia Italy
Phone: +39 04 15223812

#59
A Beccafico
Cuisines: Italian
Address: Campo San Stefano 2801
30124 Venezia Italy
Phone: +39 04 15274879

#60
Quadri
Cuisines: European
Address: Piazza San Marco 121
30124 Venezia Italy
Phone: +39 04 15222105

#61
Osteria AL Portego
di Pelliccioli Riccardo
Cuisines: Italian
Address: Via Castello 6014
30122 Venezia Italy
Phone: +39 04 15229038

#62
Al Nono Risorto
Cuisines: Italian, Seafood
Address: Calle della Regina 2337
30135 Venezia Italy
Phone: +39 04 15241161

#63
Osteria da Fiore
Cuisines: Italian
Address: Sestiere San Polo 2273A
30125 Venezia Italy
Phone: +39 04 1710104

#64
Cantinone Storico
Cuisines: Italian
Address: Fondamenta Bragadin
30123 Venezia Italy
Phone: +39 04 15239577

#65
Antico Dolo
Cuisines: Venetian
Address: Sestiere San Polo 778
30125 Venezia Italy
Phone: +39 04 15226546

#66
Ribot
Cuisines: Italian
Address: Santa Croce 158
30133 Venezia Italy
Phone: +39 04 15242486

#67
L'Anice Stellato
Cuisines: Italian
Address: Fondamenta de la Sensa
30121 Venezia Italy
Phone: +39 04 1720744

#68
Ristorante Giorgione
Cuisines: Venetian, Seafood
Address: Via Garibaldi 1533
30122 Venezia Italy
Phone: +39 04 15228727

#69
La Taverna
Cuisines: Italian
Address: Canareggio 5701
30122 Venezia Italy
Phone: +39 04 1522878

#70
La Colombina
Cuisines: Italian
Address: Sestiere Cannaregio 1828
30121 Venezia Italy
Phone: +39 04 15222616

#71
Trattoria Rivetta
Cuisines: Italian
Address: Castello 4625 Venezia Italy
Phone: +39 04 15287302

#72
San Trovaso
Cuisines: Italian
Address: Dorsoduro 967
30100 Venezia Italy
Phone: +39 04 15230835

#73
Ristorante Grand Canal
Cuisines: Italian
Address: San Marco 1332
30124 Venezia Italy
Phone: +39 04 15200211

#74
Bacarando in Corte dell' Orso
Cuisines: Italian
Address: San Marco 5495
30124 Venezia Italy
Phone: +39 04 15238280

#75
Antico Martini
Cuisines: Italian
Address: Campo Teatro Fenice 2007
30124 Venezia Italy
Phone: +39 04 15224121

#76
Osteria alla Botte
Cuisines: Italian
Address: San Marco 5482 Venezia Italy
Phone: +39 04 15209775

#77
Ristorante San Stefano
Cuisines: Italian
Address: Campo San Stefano 2776
30124 Venezia Italy
Phone: +39 04 15232467

#78
Trattoria da Alvise
Cuisines: Pizza
Address: Zona Cannaregio 5045A
30121 Venezia Italy
Phone: +39 04 18122263

#79
Gam Gam
Cuisines: Italian, Kosher
Address: Cannaregio 1122
30121 Venezia Italy
Phone: +39 417 15284

#80
Terrazza Danieli
Cuisines: Italian
Address: Castello 4196
30122 Venezia Italy
Phone: +39 04 15226480

#81
Da Mario Alla Fava
Cuisines: Italian
Address: Sestiere San Marco 5242
30124 Venezia Italy
Phone: +39 04 15285147

#82
All' Arco
Cuisines: Italian
Address: San Polo 436
30125 Venezia Italy
Phone: +39 04 15205666

#83
Da Poggi
Cuisines: Italian, Wine Bar
Address: Rio Terà de la Madalena 2103
30121 Venezia Italy
Phone: +39 04 1721199

#84
Ae Oche
Cuisines: Italian
Address: Calle del Tintor 1552
30122 Venezia Italy
Phone: +39 04 15241161

#85
Antico Gafaro
Cuisines: Venetian
Address: Sestiere Santa Croce 116
30135 Venezia Italy
Phone: +39 04 15242823

#86
Ostaria al Vecio Pozzo
Cuisines: Italian
Address: Santa Croce 656
30135 Venezia Italy
Phone: +39 04 15242760

#87
Al Giardinetto
Cuisines: Venetian
Address: Castello 4928
30122 Venezia Italy
Phone: +39 04 15285332

#88
Ai Gondolieri
Cuisines: Italian
Address: Dorsoduro 366
30100 Venezia Italy
Phone: +39 04 15286396

#89
Osteria Ae Sconte
Cuisines: Italian, Seafood
Address: Castello 5533
30122 Venezia Italy
Phone: +39 04 15239592

#90
Trattoria Leoncini
Cuisines: Italian
Address: San Marco 352
30124 Venezia Italy
Phone: +39 04 12960810

#91
Oniga
Cuisines: Italian
Address: Dorsoduro, 2852
30123 Venezia Italy
Phone: +39 04 15224410

#92
Linea d' Ombra
Cuisines: Seafood
Address: Dorsoduro 19
30123 Venezia Italy
Phone: +39 04 12411881

#93
Fritto Inn
Cuisines: Italian
Address: Cannaregio 1587
30121 Venezia Italy
Phone: +39 333 5979818

#94
Da Luca e Fred
Cuisines: Italian
Address: Rio Tera San Leonardo
30121 Venezia Italy
Phone: +39 04 1716170

#95
Mistra
Cuisines: Italian
Address: Sestiere Giudecca 212A
30133 Venezia Italy
Phone: +39 04 15220743

#96
Osteria Antico Giardinetto
Cuisines: Italian
Address: Sestiere San Croce 2253
30135 Venezia Italy
Phone: +39 04 1722882

#97
Da Ivo
Cuisines: Italian
Address: Sestiere San Marco 1809
30124 Venezia Italy
Phone: +39 04 15285004

#98
Corner Pub
Cuisines: Pub, Sandwiches
Address: Calle Della Chiesa 684 Venezia
Italy
Phone: +39 03 299176561

#99
Antico Dolo
Cuisines: Bar, Cucina Campana
Address: Ruga Vecchia San Giovanni 778
30125 Venezia Italy
Phone: +39 04 15226546

#100
Il Nuovo Galeon
di G. Galardi e D. Sabadin
Cuisines: Italian
Address: Sestiere Castello 1308
30122 Venezia Italy
Phone: +39 04 15204656

#101
Pronto Pesce
Cuisines: Seafood, Italian
Address: San Polo 319
30125 Venezia Italy
Phone: +39 04 18220298

#102
Quanto Basta
Cuisines: Desserts, Kebab, Pizza
Address: Cannaregio 148
30121 Venezia Italy
Phone: +39 04 15242939

#103
Anima Bella
Cuisines: Italian
Address: San Marco, 956
30124 Venezia Italy
Phone: +39 04 15227486

#104
Dolce Freddo
Cuisines: Italian, Ice Cream
Address: Calle delle Bande 5377
30122 Venezia Italy
Phone: +39 03 415206215

#105
Alle Zattere Pizzeria Michele
Cuisines: Pizza
Address: Via Dorsoduro 795
30123 Venezia Italy
Phone: +39 04 15204224

#106
Ca' Bonvicini
Cuisines: Bar, Italian, Coffee & Tea
Address: Santa Croce
30124 Venezia Italy
Phone: +39 04 12750106

#107
Pizzerie Ae Oche
Cuisines: Pizza, Italian
Address: Dorsoduro 1414
30100 Venezia Italy
Phone: +39 04 15206601

#108
GelatiNico
Cuisines: Italian, Ice Cream
Address: Dorsoduro 922
30123 Venezia Italy
Phone: +39 444 15225293

#109
Trattoria ai Carazzieri
Cuisines: Italian
Address: Sestiere Castello 39
30122 Venezia Italy
Phone: +39 04 15289859

#110
Osteria Da Rioba
Cuisines: Italian
Address: 2553 Cannaregio
30121 Venezia Italy
Phone: +39 04 15244379

#111
Osteria da Alberto
Cuisines: Italian
Address: Calle Larga Giacinto
Gallina 5401 Venezia Italy
Phone: +39 04 15238153

#112
A La Vecia Cavana
Cuisines: Seafood
Address: Rio Tera SS.
Apostoli Venezia Italy
Phone: +39 04 15287106

#113
Antica Trattoria La Furatola
Cuisines: Italian
Address: Sestiere Dorsoduro 2870
30100 Venezia Italy
Phone: +39 04 15201192

#114
Hosteria Al Rusteghi
Cuisines: Italian, Wine Bar
Address: Sestiere San Marco 5529
30124 Venezia Italy
Phone: +39 04 15232205

#115
Trattoria Da Silvio
Cuisines: Italian
Address: San Pantalon 3748
30100 Venezia Italy
Phone: +39 04 15205833

#116
Da Franz
Cuisines: Italian
Address: Fondamenta San Giuseppe 754
30122 Venezia Italy
Phone: +39 04 12419278

#117
Osteria Bentigodi da Andrea
Cuisines: Italian
Address: Cannaregio 1423
30121 Venezia Italy
Phone: +39 04 1716269

#118
Pasticceria Alla Bragora
Cuisines: Cafe
Address: Salizada Sant' Antonin 3604
30122 Venezia Italy
Phone: +39 04 15227579

#119
I Figli Delle Stelle
Cuisines: Italian
Address: Isola Giudecca 71
30133 Venezia Italy
Phone: +39 04 15230004

#120
Gino's Past and Pizza
Cuisines: Venetian
Address: Lista di Spagna
30121 Venezia Italy
Phone: +39 04 171607

#121
Trattoria Chinellato
Cuisines: Italian
Address: Via Castello 4227
30122 Venezia Italy
Phone: +39 04 15236025

#122
Osteria del Cason
Cuisines: Wine Bar, Seafood, Venetian
Address: San Polo 2925
30125 Venezia Italy
Phone: +39 04 12440060

#123
Ostaria al Ponte
Cuisines: Italian, Pub
Address: Sestiere Cannaregio 6369
30121 Venezia Italy
Phone: +39 04 15286157

#124
Al 40 Ladroni
Cuisines: Italian
Address: Sestiere Cannaregio, 3253
30121 Venezia Italy
Phone: +39 04 1715736

#125
Trattoria Da Fiore
Cuisines: Italian
Address: Stanto Stefano 3461
30124 Venezia Italy
Phone: +39 04 15235310

#126
Al Vecio Canton
Cuisines: Pizza, Venetian
Address: Sestiere Castello 4738A
30122 Venezia Italy
Phone: +39 04 15287143

#127
Falciani
Cuisines: Italian
Address: San Marco 353
30124 Venezia Italy
Phone: +39 04 15224872

#128
Cucina da Mario
Cuisines: Italian
Address: San Marco 2614
30124 Venezia Italy
Phone: +39 04 15285968

#129
Osteria Alba Nova
Cuisines: Italian
Address: Santa Croce 1252
30135 Venezia Italy
Phone: +39 04 15241353

#130
Trattoria Pizzeria
Cuisines: Italian
Address: Cannaregio 5045 A 30131
30121 Venezia Italy
Phone: +39 04 15204185

#131
Al Fontego
Cuisines: Italian
Address: Calle Priuli o Calle La Racheta
30121 Venezia Italy
Phone: +39 09 05200538

#132
Torrefazione Marche
Cuisines: Cafe
Address: Cannaregio 1337
30121 Venezia Italy
Phone: +39 04 1716371

#133
Ostaria Ale DoMarie
Cuisines: Italian
Address: Castello 3129
30122 Venezia Italy
Phone: +39 04 12960424

#134
Al Carbon
Cuisines: Italian
Address: San Marco 4643
30100 Venezia Italy
Phone: +39 04 15285101

#135
Pizzaway
Cuisines: Italian
Address: Rio Marin 890
30135 Venezia Italy
Phone: +39 417 16636

#136
La Terrazza
Cuisines: Italian
Address: Sestiere San Marco 4423
30124 Venezia Italy
Phone: +39 04 15236468

#137
Osteria da Codroma
Cuisines: Venetian
Address: Dorsodoro 2540
30123 Venezia Italy
Phone: +39 04 15246789

#138
Osteria Al Ponte La Patatina
Cuisines: Venetian
Address: San Polo 2741 A
30100 Venezia Italy
Phone: +39 04 15237238

#139
Trattoria da Bepi
Cuisines: Italian, Bistro
Address: Via Cannaregio 4550
30121 Venezia Italy
Phone: +39 04 15285031

#140
Pizzeria La Perla
Cuisines: Pizza
Address: Sestiere Cannaregio, 4615
30121 Venezia Italy
Phone: +39 04 15285175

#141
Muro Venezia Frari
Cuisines: Italian
Address: Sestiere San Polo 2604
30125 Venezia Italy
Phone: +39 04 12412339

#142
Osteria al Diavolo e l'Acquasanta
Cuisines: Italian
Address: Salita San Polo 561B
30125 Venezia Italy
Phone: +39 04 12770307

#143
Osteria Al DO Farai
Cuisines: Italian
Address: Sestiere Dorsoduro 3278
30123 Venezia Italy
Phone: +39 04 12770369

#144
Trattoria Antica Bessetta
Cuisines: Italian
Address: Sestiere Santa Croce 1395
30124 Venezia Italy
Phone: +39 04 1721687

#145
Al Mercanti
Cuisines: Italian
Address: Sestiere San Marco 4346A
30124 Venezia Italy
Phone: +39 04 15238269

#146
Brek
Cuisines: Italian
Address: Cannaregio 124
30121 Venezia Italy
Phone: +39 412 440158

#147
Santo Stefano
Cuisines: Italian, Pizza
Address: Via San Marco 2776
30124 Venezia Italy
Phone: +39 04 15232467

#148
La Rivista
Cuisines: Italian
Address: Dorsoduro 979
30100 Venezia Italy
Phone: +39 04 12401425

#149
McDonald's
Cuisines: Burgers
Address: Cannaregio 3922
30121 Venezia Italy
Phone: +39 04 15222969

#150
Al Paradisio
Cuisines: Italian
Address: Calle dei Paradiso
30122 Venezia Italy
Phone: +39 04 1523491

#151
Anima Bella
Cuisines: Italian
Address: San Marco 956
30124 Venezia Italy
Phone: +39 04 15227486

#152
Fiaschetteria Toscana
Cuisines: Italian
Address: Strada Cannaregio 5719
30121 Venezia Italy
Phone: +39 04 15285281

#153
Osteria al Garanghelo
Cuisines: Italian
Address: San Polo 1570 Calle dei Boteri
30125 Venezia Italy
Phone: +39 04 1721721

#154
Osteria alla Bifora
Cuisines: Italian
Address: Campo Santa Margherita
30123 Venezia Italy
Phone: +39 04 15236119

#155
Osteria Ristoteca Oniga
Cuisines: Italian
Address: Campo San Barnaba
30100 Venezia Italy
Phone: +39 04 15224410

#156
Muro Venezia Rialto
Cuisines: Bar, Italian, Canteen
Address: San Polo 222
30135 Venezia Italy
Phone: +39 04 12412339

#157
Ostaria Ae Botti
Cuisines: Venetian
Address: 609 Giudecca
30133 Venezia Italy
Phone: +39 04 12412200

#158
Antica Osteria Ruga Rialto
Cuisines: Mediterranean, Sandwiches
Address: Centro Storico calle del Sturion
692 30125 Venezia Italy
Phone: +39 04 15211243

#159
Bar Cupido
Cuisines: Pizza
Address: Cannaregio 5042
30121 Venezia Italy
Phone: +39 390 415235687

#160
Osteria a la Campana
Cuisines: Italian
Address: Calle dei fabbri 4720
30124 Venezia Italy
Phone: +39 04 15285170

#161
Pier Dickens
Cuisines: Pizza
Address: Dorsoduro 3410
30123 Venezia Italy
Phone: +39 04 12411979

#162
Rio Novo
Cuisines: Italian, Pizza
Address: Santa Croce 278
30135 Venezia Italy
Phone: +39 04 1711007

#163
la Bella Pollastrella Cannaregio
Cuisines: Italian
Address: Sestiere Cannaregio 408
30121 Venezia Italy
Phone: +39 04 15227613

#164
Caffè Al Fontego
Cuisines: Sandwiches
Address: Dorsoduro 3426 Venezia Italy
Phone: +39 04 13190444

#165
Terrazza Danieli
Cuisines: Italian
Address: Riva degle Schiavoni 4196
30122 Venezia Italy
Phone: +39 04 15226480

#166
Enoteca Al Volto
Cuisines: Wine Bar, Venetian
Address: San Marco 4081 Venezia Italy
Phone: +39 04 15228945

#167
Luna Sentada
Cuisines: Asian Fusion, Italian
Address: Campo San Severo
30122 Venezia Italy
Phone: +39 134 98821488

#168
Acqua Pazza
Cuisines: Italian, Seafood
Address: Sestiere San Marco 3808
30124 Venezia Italy
Phone: +39 04 12770688

#169
Osteria BEA Vita SNC di Avologno Roberto
Cuisines: Bistro
Address: Sestiere Cannaregio, 3082
30121 Venezia Italy
Phone: +39 04 12759347

#170
Trattoria Alla Basilica
Cuisines: Italian
Address: 4255 - 4260
30121 Venezia Italy
Phone: +39 04 15220524

#171
Osteria Alba Nova Dalla Maria
Cuisines: Italian
Address: Lista Vecchia Dei Bari
Venezia Italy
Phone: +39 04 15241353

#172
Ai Quattro Rusteghi
Cuisines: Italian
Address: Cannaregio 2888
30013 Venezia Italy
Phone: +39 04 1715160

#173
Do Leoni
Cuisines: Italian
Address: Riva degli Schiavoni 4171
30122 Venezia Italy
Phone: +39 04 15200533

#174
Lineadombra
Cuisines: Venetian
Address: Dorsoduro 19
30100 Venezia Italy
Phone: +39 04 12411881

#175
Trattoria da Ignazio
Cuisines: Italian
Address: Sestiere San Polo 2749
30125 Venezia Italy
Phone: +39 04 15234852

#176
Alla Basilica
Cuisines: Venetian
Address: Calle Albanesi 4255
30122 Venezia Italy
Phone: +39 390 415220524

#177
Hosteria al Vecio Bragosso
Cuisines: Italian
Address: Strada Nuova 4386
30131 Venezia Italy
Phone: +39 01 3042010

#178
Osteria da Baco
Cuisines: Italian
Address: Calle delle Rasse
30122 Venezia Italy
Phone: +39 04 15222887

#179
Osteria Garanghelo
Cuisines: Italian
Address: Via Garibaldi 1621
30122 Venezia Italy
Phone: +39 04 15204967

#180
Canal Grande
Cuisines: Italian
Address: Rialot Riva del Vin 740
30125 Venezia Italy
Phone: +39 04 15285166

#181
Rosticceria 'San Bartolomeo
Cuisines: Italian
Address: Sestiere San Marco 5423
30124 Venezia Italy
Phone: +39 04 15223569

#182
Residenza Cannaregio
Cuisines: Hotels, Italian
Address: Cannaregio 3210/A
30121 Venezia Italy
Phone: +39 04 15244332

#183
Osteria Enoteco Ai Artisti
Cuisines: Local Flavor, Italian
Address: Fondamenta della Toletta 1169A
30123 Venezia Italy
Phone: +39 04 15238944

#184
Caffè Rosso
Cuisines: Cafe
Address: Campo Santa Margherita 2967
30123 Venezia Italy
Phone: +39 04 15287998

#185
Trattoria Pizzeria ai Fabbri
Cuisines: Venetian
Address: San Marco 4717
30124 Venezia Italy
Phone: +39 04 15208085

#186
Pane Vino e SanDaniele
Cuisines: Italian
Address: Sestiere Dorsoduro
30123 Venezia Italy
Phone: +39 04 15237456

#187
Osteria Doge Morosini
Cuisines: Italian
Address: San Marco 2958
30124 Venezia Italy
Phone: +39 04 15226922

#188
Osteria Kalia
Cuisines: Italian
Address: Calle del dose 5870
30122 Venezia Italy
Phone: +39 04 15285153

#189
Osteria da Carla
Cuisines: Venetian
Address: Frezzeria San Marco 1535
30124 Venezia Italy
Phone: +39 04 15237855

#190
Osteria Al Pozzo Roverso
Cuisines: Italian
Address: 30122 Castello
30122 Venezia Italy
Phone: +39 04 15202759

#191
Da Roberto
Cuisines: Italian
Address: Campo San Provolo 4707
30122 Venezia Italy
Phone: +39 04 15221506

#192
Sansovino
Cuisines: Pizza
Address: Sestiere San Marco 2628
30124 Venezia Italy
Phone: +39 04 15286141

#193
Hard Rock Cafe
Cuisines: Coffee & Tea
Address: Sestiere San Marco 959
30124 Venezia Italy
Phone: +39 04 15210486

#194
Vecio Fritolin
Cuisines: Italian
Address: Sestiere Santa Croce 2262
30135 Venezia Italy
Phone: +39 04 15222881

#195
Osteria ae Cravate
Cuisines: Italian
Address: Santa Croce 36
30135 Venezia Italy
Phone: +39 04 15287912

#196
Devis
Cuisines: Italian
Address: Sestiere Cannaregio 55
30121 Venezia Italy
Phone: +39 04 1715023

#197
La Perla
Cuisines: Italian
Address: Cannaregio 4615
30121 Venezia Italy
Phone: +39 04 15285175

#198
Osteria ae Botti
Cuisines: Venetian
Address: Giudecca Santa Eufemia 609
30133 Venezia Italy
Phone: +39 04 17241086

#199
Le Maschere
Cuisines: Italian
Address: San Marco 760
30124 Venezia Italy
Phone: +39 04 15236791

#200
Osteria Giorgione
Cuisines: Italian
Address: Sestiere Cannaregio 4582A
30121 Venezia Italy
Phone: +39 04 15221725

#201
Zanzibar
Cuisines: Cafe, Bar
Address: Campo Santa Maria Formosa
30122 Venezia Italy
Phone: +39 347 1460107

#202
La Lista Bistro
Cuisines: Deli, Breakfast & Brunch
Address: Cannaregio 225A
30121 Venezia Italy
Phone: +39 04 15244098

#203
**Trattoria Dona Onesta
di Salama Safwat**
Cuisines: Bistro
Address: Sestiere Dorsoduro 3922
30100 Venezia Italy
Phone: +39 04 10997972

#204
Pedrocchi
Cuisines: Italian
Address: Via Cannareggio 278A
30121 Venezia Italy
Phone: +39 04 10997864

#205
Taverna Da Baffo
Cuisines: Italian
Address: San Polo 2346
30125 Venezia Italy
Phone: +39 04 15242061

#206
Alla Basilica
Cuisines: Italian
Address: Calle Degli Albanesi 4255
30122 Venezia Italy
Phone: +39 04 15220524

#207
La Mela Verde
Cuisines: Ice Cream, Coffee & Tea
Address: Fondamenta de l'Osmarin
30030 Venezia Italy
Phone: +39 349 1957924

#208
Pizzeria Venezia
Cuisines: Italian, Seafood
Address: Viale Amerigo Vespucci 30
54033 Venezia Italy
Phone: +39 05 85634453

#209
Cantina do Spade
Cuisines: Italian
Address: San Polo 859
30124 Venezia Italy
Phone: +39 04 15210583

#210
Le Coccinelle
Cuisines: Pizza, Italian
Address: Santa Croce 284
30135 Venezia Italy
Phone: +39 03 655260275

#211
Al Vecio Bragosso
Cuisines: Seafood, Venetian
Address: Cannaregio 4385
30121 Venezia Italy
Phone: +39 04 15237277

#212
Al Canton del Gallo
Cuisines: Cafe
Address: Gran Viale Santa Maria
Elisabetta 14 Venezia Italy
Phone: +39 04 15260358

#213
Cicchetteria
Cuisines: Italian
Address: Sestiere San Polo 860
30125 Venezia Italy
Phone: +39 04 15210583

#214
Trattoria do Forni
Cuisines: Italian, Bistro
Address: Sestiere San Marco 457
30124 Venezia Italy
Phone: +39 04 15237729

#215
Hotel Metropole
Cuisines: Italian
Address: Riva degli Schiavoni 4149
30122 Venezia Italy
Phone: +39 04 15205044

#216
Biennale
Cuisines: Italian
Address: Sestiere Castello 1775
30122 Venezia Italy
Phone: +39 04 15284323

#217
Da Fiore
Cuisines: Italian
Address: Sestiere San Polo 2002
30125 Venezia Italy
Phone: +39 04 1721343

#218
Sapori Venexiani
Cuisines: Italian, Seafood
Address: Calle del Dose Castello 5870A
30122 Venezia Italy
Phone: +39 04 12411991

#219
Aciugheta
Cuisines: Sandwiches
Address: Sestiere Castello, 4357
30122 Venezia Italy
Phone: +39 04 15224292

#220
Antico Gatoleto
Cuisines: Seafood, Venetian, Pizza
Address: Sestiere Cannaregio 6055
30131 Venezia Italy
Phone: +39 04 15221883

#221
Al Brindisi
Cuisines: Italian
Address: Campo San Geremio 307
30100 Venezia Italy
Phone: +39 04 1716968

#222
Antico Pignolo
Cuisines: Italian
Address: Sestiere San Marco 451
30124 Venezia Italy
Phone: +39 04 15228123

#223
Harry's Bar
Cuisines: Bar, Italian
Address: Sestiere San Marco 1323
30124 Venezia Italy
Phone: +39 04 15285777

#224
Al Sportivi
Cuisines: Italian
Address: Dorsoduro 3052
30123 Venezia Italy
Phone: +39 415 211598

#225
Artblu Cafe
Cuisines: Italian
Address: Campo Santo Stefano 2808
30124 Venezia Italy
Phone: +39 347 7504466

#226
Giuge Federico
Cuisines: Italian
Address: Calle Chinotto Generale 24
30132 Venezia Italy
Phone: +39 04 15208419

#227
Ristorante Omnibus
Cuisines: Italian
Address: San Marco Riva Del Carbon 4171
30124 Venezia Italy
Phone: +39 04 15237213

#228
Alle Lanternine
Cuisines: Italian
Address: Campiello Chiesa
30121 Venezia Italy
Phone: +39 04 15244570

#229
Ai Scalzi
Cuisines: Italian
Address: Sestiere Cannaregio 59/60
30121 Venezia Italy
Phone: +39 04 1715023

#230
Naranzaria
Cuisines: Italian
Address: San Polo 130
30125 Venezia Italy
Phone: +39 04 17241035

#231
Pizzeria Marco Polo
Cuisines: Italian
Address: Sestiere castello 5571
30122 Venezia Italy
Phone: +39 04 15235018

#232
All'Aquila
Cuisines: Italian
Address: Rio Terrà Lista di Spagna
30121 Venezia Italy
Phone: +39 04 1715707

#233
Trattoria Rialto Novo
Cuisines: Italian
Address: Sestiere San Polo 518
30125 Venezia Italy
Phone: +39 04 15235774

#234
La Porta D'Acqua
Cuisines: Mediterranean,
Seafood, Cucina Campana
Address: Rio Terà San Silvestro 1022B
30125 Venezia Italy
Phone: +39 04 12412124

#235
Inishark
Cuisines: Irish, Pub
Address: Sestiere Castello 5787
30122 Venezia Italy
Phone: +39 04 15235300

#236
Trattoria Ai Tre Ponti
Cuisines: Bistro
Address: Sestiere Santa Croce 271
30135 Venezia Italy
Phone: +39 04 12750619

#237
Papadopoli
Cuisines: Italian
Address: Sestiere San Croce 245
30135 Venezia Italy
Phone: +39 04 1720924

#238
**CIP Ciap La Bottega Della Pizza
SNC / Piergiorgio**
Cuisines: Pizza
Address: Via Castello, 5799/A
30010 Venezia Italy
Phone: +39 04 15236621

#239
HK Venezia
Cuisines: Italian, Wine Bar
Address: Sestiere di San Marco
30124 Venezia Italy
Phone: +39 04 12743614

#240
Da Nino
Cuisines: Coffee & Tea
Address: Sestiere Santa Croce 565
30135 Venezia Italy
Phone: +39 04 1718955

#241
Conca D'oro SAS
di Giuseppe Costa
Cuisines: Pizza
Address: Sestiere Castello, 4338
30122 Venezia Italy
Phone: +39 04 15285686

#242
Arte della Pizza
Cuisines: Pizza
Address: Sestiere Cannaregio 1861
30131 Venezia Italy
Phone: +39 04 15246520

#243
Alberghi Hotel Concordia
Cuisines: Italian
Address: Sestiere San Marco 367
30100 Venezia Italy
Phone: +39 04 15206866

#244
Al Conte Pescaor
Cuisines: Italian
Address: San Marco 544
30125 Venezia Italy
Phone: +39 04 15221483

#245
Aromi
Cuisines: Italian
Address: Giudecca 810
30133 Venezia Italy
Phone: +39 04 12723311

#246
Bacaro Risorto
Cuisines: Wine Bar, Coffee & Tea
Address: Campo San Provolo
4700 Venezia Italy
Phone: +39 04 15287274

#247
Alberghi: Hotel Gritti Palace
Cuisines: Italian
Address: Sestiere San Marco 2467
30124 Venezia Italy
Phone: +39 04 1794611

#248
Bar All'Orologio
Cuisines: Pizza, Sandwiches, Venetian
Address: Castello 6130
30122 Venezia Italy
Phone: +39 04 15230515

#249
Trattoria Dalla Marisa
Cuisines: Venetian
Address: Cannaregio 652
30121 Venezia Italy
Phone: +39 04 1720211

#250
Al Vecio Calice
Cuisines: Bistro, Italian
Address: Castello 1664
30122 Venezia Italy
Phone: +39 339 8074213

#251
Bacco Felice
Cuisines: Italian
Address: Santa Croce 197E
30135 Venezia Italy
Phone: +39 415 287794

#252
Trattoria Pizzeria
da Paolo / Fabiana
Cuisines: Pizza
Address: Sestiere Castello, 2389
30122 Venezia Italy
Phone: +39 04 15210660

#253
Ostaria al Garanghelo
Cuisines: Italian
Address: San Polo 1570
30125 Venezia Italy
Phone: +39 04 1721721

#254
Dalla Mora
Cuisines: Italian
Address: Fondamenta Daniele Manin 75
30141 Venezia Italy
Phone: +39 04 15274606

#255
Bacaromi
Cuisines: Italian
Address: Giudecca 810
30132 Venezia Italy
Phone: +39 04 12723311

#256
Pizzeria Tre Archi
Cuisines: Bar, Pizza
Address: Via Cannaregio 552
30121 Venezia Italy
Phone: +39 04 1716438

#257
Avogaria
Cuisines: Italian
Address: Sestiere Dorsoduro 1629
30123 Venezia Italy
Phone: +39 04 12960491

#258
iL Refolo
Cuisines: Italian, Pizza
Address: Santa Croce 1459
30124 Venezia Italy
Phone: +39 04 15240016

#259
Osteria di Cravatte
Cuisines: Italian
Address: Santa Croce 36
30135 Venezia Italy
Phone: +39 04 15287912

#260
Venissa
Cuisines: Italian
Address: Fondamenta Santa Caterina 3
30121 Venezia Italy
Phone: +39 04 15272281

#261
Trattoria Agli Artisti da Piero
Cuisines: Italian
Address: Ruga Giuffa 4835
30122 Venezia Italy
Phone: +39 04 12412312

#262
Ristoranti: La Gondola
Cuisines: Italian
Address: Sestiere Castello 4611
30122 Venezia Italy
Phone: +39 04 15224097

#263
Terrazza Del Casin dei Nobili
Cuisines: Italian
Address: Venezia Zattere Dorsoduro 924
30123 Venezia Italy
Phone: +39 04 15206895

#264
Da Stephano
Cuisines: Pizza, Italian
Address: San Marco 2953
30124 Venezia Italy
Phone: +39 04 15232467

#265
Le Cafe
Cuisines: Italian
Address: Campo San Stefano 2797
30124 Venezia Italy
Phone: +39 390 415237201

#266
Conca D'oro S.a.s.
di Costa Giovanbattista C.
Cuisines: Pizza
Address: Sestiere Castello 4338
30122 Venezia Italy
Phone: +39 04 15229293

#267
Da GIOSIA
Cuisines: Wine Bar, Sandwiches
Address: Santa Croce 458X
30135 Venezia Italy
Phone: +39 329 0771340

#268
Ancora Venezia
Cuisines: Venetian
Address: Campo di San Giacometto
30125 Venezia Italy
Phone: +39 04 15207066

#269
Caffe' del Doge
Cuisines: Bar, Coffee & Tea
Address: Sestiere Castello 5197
30122 Venezia Italy
Phone: +39 04 12411949

#270
Bar Americano
Cuisines: Venetian
Address: San Marco 30A
30124 Venezia Italy
Phone: +39 04 15222515

#271
Caffe La Piscina
Cuisines: Italian
Address: Dorsoduro 782
30100 Venezia Italy
Phone: +39 04 15206466

#272
La Piazzetta
Cuisines: Italian
Address: Calle Larga San Marco
30124 Venezia Italy
Phone: +39 04 15206866

#273
A Beccafico Arte
Cuisines: Italian
Address: Strada Nuova Cannaregio 2289C
30121 Venezia Italy
Phone: +39 04 12759220

#274
Osteria Al Squero
Cuisines: Tapas
Address: Dorsoduro 943
30100 Venezia Italy
Phone: +39 335 6007513

#275
Osteria Da Filo
Cuisines: Italian
Address: Calle Tintor Cannaregio
Venezia Italy
Phone: +39 04 98601562

#276
Conca D'Oro
Cuisines: Italian
Address: Sestiere Castello 4338
30122 Venezia Italy
Phone: +39 04 15229293

#277
La Rossa Dei Venti
Cuisines: Italian
Address: Fondamenta Condulmer
Venezia Italy
Phone: +39 04 12440083

#278
Autorimessa
Cuisines: Italian
Address: Sestiere San Croce 497
30135 Venezia Italy
Phone: +39 04 15200486

#279
Bar: Al Leon D'oro
Cuisines: Coffee & Tea
Address: Via Cannaregio 2345
30121 Venezia Italy
Phone: +39 04 1720693

#280
Il Migliore
Cuisines: Italian
Address: Fondamenta Misericordia
30121 Venezia Italy
Phone: +39 04 15230607

#281
Aquil Nera
Cuisines: Food, Italian
Address: 5301 Venezia
30124 Venezia Italy
Phone: +39 04 15224769

#282
Osteria dal Riccio Peoco
Cuisines: Italian
Address: Sestiere Cannaregio 4462
30122 Venezia Italy
Phone: +39 04 12410162

#283
L'alcova
Cuisines: Italian
Address: Ca' Sagredo Hotel
Campo Santa Sofia 4198
30121 Venezia Italy
Phone: +39 04 12413111

#284
Pizzería Aoeche
Cuisines: Pizza
Address: Santa Croce 1552
30124 Venezia Italy
Phone: +39 415 241161

#285
Hard Rock Cafe Italy
Cuisines: Burgers, American, Bar
Address: Sestiere S. Marco, 1192
30124 Venezia Italy
Phone: +39 04 15229665

#286
Pizzeria Le Piramidi
Cuisines: Pizza
Address: Castello 6342
30122 Venezia Italy
Phone: +39 04 15200474

#287
Da Gianni
Cuisines: Italian, Bistro
Address: Via Cannaregio 4377
30121 Venezia Italy
Phone: +39 04 15237268

#288
Antico Pizzo Risorto
Cuisines: Italian
Address: San Polo 814
30100 Venezia Italy
Phone: +39 04 15231575

#289
Osteria Ai Promessi Sposi
Cuisines: Italian, Food
Address: Cannaregio Calle dell'Oca
4367 Venezia Italy
Phone: +39 04 15228609

#290
Roma
Cuisines: Italian
Address: Sestiere Cannaregio 122
30131 Venezia Italy
Phone: +39 04 1715982

#291
Centrale
Cuisines: Italian
Address: Sestiere San Marco 658
30124 Venezia Italy
Phone: +39 04 12417978

#292
Margherita
Cuisines: Italian
Address: Sestiere San Marco 1075
30124 Venezia Italy
Phone: +39 04 15230624

#293
Mercurio
Cuisines: Italian
Address: Sestiere San Marco 3648
30124 Venezia Italy
Phone: +39 04 12412785

#294
Al Vecio Forner
Cuisines: Italian
Address: Dorsodura 671A
30123 Venezia Italy
Phone: +39 04 15280424

#295
Al Coghi
Cuisines: Pizza
Address: Via Sestiere San Polo 1022
30125 Venezia Italy
Phone: +39 04 15227307

#296
Alla Rampa Osteria Con Cucina Di Ronchiato Annamaria
Cuisines: Bistro
Address: Sre Castello 1135
Venezia Italy
Phone: +39 04 15285365

#297
Mondo Novo
Cuisines: Italian
Address: Sestiere Castello 5428
30122 Venezia Italy
Phone: +39 04 15200698

#298
AL Paradiso
Cuisines: Italian
Address: Sestiere San Polo 767
30125 Venezia Italy
Phone: +39 04 15234910

#299
BAR Cavatappi
Cuisines: Bar, Italian
Address: Sestiere San Marco 525
30124 Venezia Italy
Phone: +39 04 12960252

#300
Taverna de Remer
Cuisines: Italian
Address: Calle de la Posta de Fiorenza 5650 30121 Venezia Italy
Phone: +39 415 228789

#301
Taverna Ciardi di Armando Ciardi
Cuisines: Italian
Address: Via Calle DE L'aseo 1885
30121 Venezia Italy
Phone: +39 04 15241026

#302
La Rosa
Cuisines: Italian
Address: Santa Croce 164
30124 Venezia Italy
Phone: +39 04 12440083

#303
Gam Gam
Cuisines: Kosher
Address: Ghetto Vecchio 1122
30121 Venice Italy
Phone: +39 04 15231495

#304
**Al Graspo de Ua
Restaurant Lounge**
Cuisines: Lounge, Venetian
Address: Sestiere S.Marco 5094/A
30124 Venezia Italy
Phone: +39 04 10988030

#305
Osteria Barababao
Cuisines: Italian
Address: Campo San Giovanni
Grisostomo 5835
30121 Venezia Italy
Phone: +39 349 8778019

#306
Brek
Cuisines: Italian
Address: Sestiere Cannaregio 124
30131 Venezia Italy
Phone: +39 04 12440158

#307
Le Cafe
Cuisines: Coffee & Tea
Address: Campo San Stefano 2797
30124 Venezia Italy
Phone: +39 04 15229760

#308
Impronta Cafe
Cuisines: Italian
Address: Dorsoduro 3815
30100 Venezia Italy
Phone: +39 04 12750386

#309
Beppino
Cuisines: Italian, Pizza
Address: Sestriere di San Marco 416
30124 Venezia Italy
Phone: +39 04 15230718

#310
Pizzeria Trattoria Vesuvio
Cuisines: Bar, Italian
Address: Sestiere Cannaregio 1837
30121 Venezia Italy
Phone: +39 04 1795688

#311
Trattoria San Toma
Cuisines: Italian
Address: Campo San Toma
30125 Venezia Italy
Phone: +39 04 15238819

#312
Al Giglio
Cuisines: Specialty Food, Italian
Address: San Marco 2477
30124 Venezia Italy
Phone: +39 04 15232368

#313
Tiozzo / Luciano
Cuisines: Deli
Address: Sestiere Castello, 4833
30122 Venezia Italy
Phone: +39 04 15230294

#314
Twiga
Cuisines: Italian
Address: Sestiere Dorsoduro 19
30123 Venezia Italy
Phone: +39 04 12411881

#315
Rialto
Cuisines: Italian
Address: Sestiere San Marco 5148
30124 Venezia Italy
Phone: +39 04 15229222

#316
Trattoria Bella Venezia
Cuisines: Italian
Address: Sestiere Cannaregio, 129
30131 Venezia Italy
Phone: +39 04 1715208

#317
Trattoria Alla Fonte
Cuisines: Italian
Address: Castello 3820
30122 Venezia Italy
Phone: +39 415 238698

#318
Rosa Salva
Cuisines: Cafe, Ice Cream,
Desserts, Coffee & Tea
Address: Castello 6779
30122 Venezia Italy
Phone: +39 04 15227949

#319
Osteria Al Sacro e Profano
Cuisines: Italian
Address: San Polo 502
30125 Venezia Italy
Phone: +39 04 15237924

#320
Osteria da Bepi
Cuisines: Italian, Bistro
Address: Via Cannaregio 337
30121 Venezia Italy
Phone: +39 04 1716039

#321
Al Calice
Cuisines: Venetian
Address: San Marco 1502
30100 Venezia Italy
Phone: +39 04 15236318

#322
Trattoria All'Antica Mola
Cuisines: Italian
Address: Via Cannaregio 2800
30100 Venezia Italy
Phone: +39 04 1710768

#323
Tiago
Cuisines: Italian
Address: Via Dorsoduro 2344
30123 Venezia Italy
Phone: +39 04 12412697

#324
San Trovaso
Cuisines: Italian
Address: Via Dorsoduro 967
30125 Venezia Italy
Phone: +39 04 15230835

#325
Trattoria Ca' Foscari al Canton
Cuisines: Italian
Address: Sestiere Dorsoduro 3854
30123 Venezia Italy
Phone: +39 04 15229216

#326
Chen WEI
Cuisines: Chinese
Address: Via Sestiere Castello 4294
30010 Venezia Italy
Phone: +39 04 15225331

#327
**Macellerie Maso SNC di Carlo,
Narciso, Luca e UGO Maso**
Cuisines: Deli
Address: Sestiere Castello, 3825
30122 Venezia Italy
Phone: +39 04 15224773

#328
Bisiol / Maria Teresa
Cuisines: Deli
Address: Sestiere Cannaregio, 4441
30121 Venezia Italy
Phone: +39 04 15221183

#329
Veneta Ristorazione
Cuisines: Italian
Address: Via Sestiere San Marco 4697
30122 Venezia Italy
Phone: +39 04 15212665

#330
Pizzeria Al Bari
Cuisines: Pizza
Address: Sestiere Santa Croce 1175
30100 Venezia Italy
Phone: +39 04 1718900

#331
Regalini Lucio
Cuisines: Deli
Address: Sestiere San Croce 892
30135 Venezia Italy
Phone: +39 04 1718602

#332
Hotel Salieri
Cuisines: Italian
Address: Sestiere San Croce 160
30135 Venezia Italy
Phone: +39 04 1721246

#333
Remax
Cuisines: Italian
Address: Sestiere Dorsoduro 2870
30123 Venezia Italy
Phone: +39 04 15208594

#334
Trattoria AL Gazzettino
Cuisines: Italian
Address: Sestiere San Marco 4972
30124 Venezia Italy
Phone: +39 04 15210497

#335
Al Theatro
Cuisines: Pizza
Address: Sestiere San Marco 1917
30124 Venezia Italy
Phone: +39 04 15221052

#336
Santo Stefano
Cuisines: Italian
Address: San Marco 2776
30124 Venezia Italy
Phone: +39 04 15232467

#337
Florida
Cuisines: Italian
Address: Sestiere San Polo 733
30125 Venezia Italy
Phone: +39 04 15226271

#338
Alberghi: Hotel Europa & Regina
Cuisines: Italian
Address: Sestiere San Marco 2159
30124 Venezia Italy
Phone: +39 04 15200477

#339
Centrale
Cuisines: Italian
Address: Sestiere San Marco 425
30124 Venezia Italy
Phone: +39 04 15205730

#340
Antares
Cuisines: Pizza
Address: Sestiere San Marco 367B
30124 Venezia Italy
Phone: +39 04 15206524

#341
Giacomin Daniele
Cuisines: Deli
Address: Sestiere San Marco 3696
30124 Venezia Italy
Phone: +39 04 15203123

#342
Margherita
Cuisines: Fast Food
Address: Sestiere S. Marco, 3726
30124 Venezia Italy
Phone: +39 04 15229498

#343
Mopi
Cuisines: Italian
Address: Sestiere San Marco 280
30124 Venezia Italy
Phone: +39 04 15209896

#344
Alla Colomba
Cuisines: Italian
Address: Sestiere San Marco 1665
30124 Venezia Italy
Phone: +39 04 15221468

#345
Colombo di Albertinelli Umberto
Cuisines: Italian
Address: Sestiere San Marco 1502
30124 Venezia Italy
Phone: +39 04 15236318

#346
La Taverna
Cuisines: Italian
Address: Sestiere San Marco 1702
30124 Venezia Italy
Phone: +39 04 15221543

#347
J M International
Cuisines: Italian
Address: Sestiere San Marco 3523
30124 Venezia Italy
Phone: +39 04 12412515

#348
Punto Pizza
Cuisines: Pizza
Address: Sestiere San Marco 553A
30124 Venezia Italy
Phone: +39 04 15208068

#349
Ste.Mi.Ro. Srl
Cuisines: Italian
Address: Sestiere San Marco 1343
30124 Venezia Italy
Phone: +39 04 12960687

#350
Da Celio
Cuisines: Italian
Address: Sestiere San Marco 375
30124 Venezia Italy
Phone: +39 04 15237216

#351
Sempione di Signora Santa
Cuisines: Italian
Address: Sestiere San Marco 578
30124 Venezia Italy
Phone: +39 04 15226022

#352
Gran Canal
Cuisines: Italian
Address: San Marco 1325
30124 Venezia Italy
Phone: +39 04 15200211

#353
Bistrot
Cuisines: Bistro
Address: Sestiere San Marco 4685
30124 Venezia Italy
Phone: +39 04 15236651

#354
Colombo
Cuisines: Italian
Address: Sestiere San Marco 2059A
30124 Venezia Italy
Phone: +39 04 15283650

#355
Venice Food & Beverage
Cuisines: Italian
Address: Sestiere San Marco 1847
30124 Venezia Italy
Phone: +39 04 15289730

#356
Eredi Baldan Piazza
Cuisines: Deli
Address: Sestiere San Marco 1160
30124 Venezia Italy
Phone: +39 04 15225833

#357
Helios di Barutti Della Vecchia Giorgio
Cuisines: Italian
Address: Sestiere San Marco 5338
30124 Venezia Italy
Phone: +39 04 15289078

#358
J.M. International
Cuisines: Italian
Address: Sestiere San Marco 2966
30124 Venezia Italy
Phone: +39 04 12770558

#359
Ubin
Cuisines: Italian
Address: Sestiere San Marco 4644
30124 Venezia Italy
Phone: +39 04 12410761

#360
Ge-Bar
Cuisines: Italian
Address: Sestiere San Marco 2477
30124 Venezia Italy
Phone: +39 04 15232368

#361
Still Novo
Cuisines: Italian
Address: Sestiere San Marco 1659B
30124 Venezia Italy
Phone: +39 04 12960664

#362
San Marco
Cuisines: Italian
Address: Sestiere San Marcon 877
30124 Venezia Italy
Phone: +39 04 15238447

#363
Giachi
Cuisines: Italian
Address: Sestiere San Marco 813
30124 Venezia Italy
Phone: +39 04 15236990

#364
La Barchessa
Cuisines: Italian
Address: Sestiere San Marco 912
30124 Venezia Italy
Phone: +39 04 15225238

#365
Battistin Antonio e Caroldi Luca
Cuisines: Deli
Address: Via Sestiere San Marco 4676
30124 Venezia Italy
Phone: +39 04 15230547

#366
Ge.Bar
Cuisines: Fast Food
Address: Sestiere San Marco 4176C
30124 Venezia Italy
Phone: +39 04 15237909

#367
Ge.Bar
Cuisines: Fast Food
Address: Sestiere San Marco 4173
30124 Venezia Italy
Phone: +39 04 15211248

#368
Marsilli Service
Cuisines: Italian
Address: Sestiere San Marco 760
30124 Venezia Italy
Phone: +39 04 15236791

#369
Petra
Cuisines: Italian
Address: Via Sestiere di San Marco 5495
30124 Venezia Italy
Phone: +39 04 15224673

#370
Alfredo Alfredo Fast Food
Cuisines: Italian
Address: Sestiere San Marco 5546
30124 Venezia Italy
Phone: +39 04 12411185

#371
Cappon / Massimo
Cuisines: Deli
Address: Sestiere Castello, 5223
30122 Venezia Italy
Phone: +39 04 15224053

#372
Fedalto Lino
Cuisines: Deli
Address: Sestiere San Polo 284
30125 Venezia Italy
Phone: +39 04 15237430

#373
Laguna Carni
Cuisines: Deli
Address: Sestiere San Polo 315
30125 Venezia Italy
Phone: +39 04 15223232

#374
Ronchi Francesco
Cuisines: Deli
Address: Sestiere San Polo 1053A
30125 Venezia Italy
Phone: +39 04 15230589

#375
D'orfeo
Cuisines: Italian
Address: Sestiere San Polo 1608
30125 Venezia Italy
Phone: +39 04 1721822

#376
Caffe' Centrale
Cuisines: Pizza
Address: Sestiere San Polo 745
30125 Venezia Italy
Phone: +39 04 15239775

#377
Centotrenta
Cuisines: Italian
Address: Sestiere San Polo 130
30125 Venezia Italy
Phone: +39 04 17241035

#378
LY S.A.S. di LU YI
Cuisines: Italian
Address: Sestiere San Polo 1588
30125 Venezia Italy
Phone: +39 04 12440293

#379
Zana
Cuisines: Pizza
Address: Sestiere San Polo 2287
30125 Venezia Italy
Phone: +39 04 1713250

#380
Perla D'oriente
Cuisines: Italian
Address: Sestiere San Polo 3004
30125 Venezia Italy
Phone: +39 04 15240398

#381
Pinto / Francesco
Cuisines: Italian
Address: Sestiere San Polo 436
30125 Venezia Italy
Phone: +39 04 15205666

#382
Rialto Carni
Cuisines: Deli
Address: Sestiere San Polo 92B
30125 Venezia Italy
Phone: +39 04 15222188

#383
Bellenzier Paola
Cuisines: Deli
Address: Via Sestiere San Polo 1472
30125 Venezia Italy
Phone: +39 04 15228433

#384
Riva
Cuisines: Italian
Address: Sestiere San Polo 677
30125 Venezia Italy
Phone: +39 04 15212694

#385
Sole
Cuisines: Italian
Address: Sestiere San Polo 731
30125 Venezia Italy
Phone: +39 04 15231164

#386
Il Giardinetto
Cuisines: Italian
Address: Sestiere San Polo 2908
30125 Venezia Italy
Phone: +39 04 15224100

#387
Bar Da Sandro
Cuisines: Pizza
Address: Sestiere San Polo 1473
30100 Venezia Italy
Phone: +39 04 15234964

#388
Riva
Cuisines: Italian
Address: Sestiere San Polo
30125 Venezia Italy
Phone: +39 04 15226397

#389
Pizzeria Peterpan
Cuisines: Pizza
Address: Via Castello, 6249
30100 Venezia Italy
Phone: +39 04 18122492

#390
Il Milion
Cuisines: Italian
Address: Via Cannaregio 5841
30131 Venezia Italy
Phone: +39 04 15229302

#391
Pizzeria Fuori Rotta
Cuisines: Italian
Address: Campo Santa Merghertia Plaza
30123 Venezia Italy
Phone: +39 04 15235640

#392
Hostaria
Cuisines: Italian
Address: Sestiere Castello 3499
30122 Venezia Italy
Phone: +39 04 15220861

#393
AL Gabbiano
Cuisines: Italian
Address: Sestiere Castello 4122
30100 Venezia Italy
Phone: +39 04 15201290

#394
Girodie
Cuisines: Italian
Address: Sestiere Castello 4088
30122 Venezia Italy
Phone: +39 04 12776072

#395
**Friggitoria Cleopatra
di Hassouna Magdi**
Cuisines: Italian
Address: Sestiere Castello 3983
30122 Venezia Italy
Phone: +39 04 15227696

#396
Gestioni Immobiliari
Cuisines: Italian
Address: Sestiere Castello 4538
30122 Venezia Italy
Phone: +39 04 17241018

#397
D.N.A.
Cuisines: Italian
Address: Sestiere Santa Croce 466
30135 Venezia Italy
Phone: +39 04 15201299

#398
Old
Cuisines: Pizza
Address: Sestiere Santa Croce 1552B
30135 Venezia Italy
Phone: +39 04 15241161

#399
Pizzaway di Amurri
Cuisines: Pizza
Address: Via Santa Croce 890
30135 Venezia Italy
Phone: +39 04 1716636

#400
Nuova Valiglia
Cuisines: Italian, Wine Bar
Address: San Marco 4697
30124 Venezia Italy
Phone: +39 04 15226330

#401
Pizzeria
Cuisines: Italian
Address: Sestiere Castello 5471
30122 Venezia Italy
Phone: +39 04 12411003

#402
Hotel Canaletto
Cuisines: Italian
Address: Castello 5487
30122 Venezia Italy
Phone: +39 04 15220518

#403
Cantina Canaletto
Cuisines: Italian
Address: Sestiere Castello 5490
30122 Venezia Italy
Phone: +39 04 12771217

#404
Vera da Pozzo
Cuisines: Italian
Address: Sestiere Castello 5530
30122 Venezia Italy
Phone: +39 04 15239592

#405
Romeo di Lotto Paola
Cuisines: Italian
Address: Sestiere Castello 5571
30122 Venezia Italy
Phone: +39 04 15235018

#406
Insieme
Cuisines: Italian
Address: Sestiere Castello 5731
30122 Venezia Italy
Phone: +39 04 15221480

#407
Ba. Ca. Ro
Cuisines: Italian
Address: Via Castello 5746
30122 Venezia Italy
Phone: +39 04 15210234

#408
Bar-Ristoranti Obillok
Cuisines: Italian
Address: Sestiere Castello 6331
30122 Venezia Italy
Phone: +39 04 15284639

#409
Pizzeria Le Piramide
Cuisines: Pizza, Italian
Address: Castello 6342
30122 Venezia Italy
Phone: +39 04 15200474

#410
DA Carletto di Ella Melk Gandi
Cuisines: Italian
Address: Via Castello 5272
30122 Venezia Italy
Phone: +39 04 15227944

#411
New Shanghai
Cuisines: Chinese
Address: Calle Priuli 101
30121 Venezia Italy
Phone: +39 04 1716232

#412
Selfservice Rialto
Cuisines: Do-It-Yourself Food, Italian
Address: Riva del Carbon
4175 San Marco Venezia Italy
Phone: +39 04 15237909

#413
T.R.A.N.I.
Cuisines: Pizza
Address: Sre Castello 6418
30122 Venezia Italy
Phone: +39 04 15203377

#414
**Panisson Mirco
& Marconi Massimo**
Cuisines: Deli
Address: Sestiere Cannaregio 1373A
30131 Venezia Italy
Phone: +39 04 1718567

#415
AL Fontego
Cuisines: Italian
Address: Sestiere Cannaregio 3711
30131 Venezia Italy
Phone: +39 04 15200538

#416
Agasson
Cuisines: Italian
Address: Via Cannaregio 2031
30121 Venezia Italy
Phone: +39 04 12004144

#417
Osteria Ale Do Marie
Cuisines: Italian
Address: Sestiere Castello 3129
30122 Venezia Italy
Phone: +39 04 12960424

#418
**Venezia Futura
di Battagliarin e Hoque**
Cuisines: Pizza
Address: Via Sestiere Dorsoduro, 3059
30123 Venezia Italy
Phone: +39 04 12412089

#419
Canal Grande
Cuisines: Italian
Address: Rival del Vin
30125 Venezia Italy
Phone: +39 04 15226271

#420
XIN Wang
Cuisines: Chinese
Address: Sestiere Cannaregio 101
30131 Venezia Italy
Phone: +39 04 1716232

#421
Tiziano Snack Bar
Cuisines: Tapas, Buffet
Address: Sestiere Cannaregio 5747
30121 Venezia Italy
Phone: +39 04 15235544

#422
Trattoria AL Campanile
Cuisines: Italian
Address: Via San Polo 2088
30125 Venezia Italy
Phone: +39 04 15237221

#423
Casa Bonita
Cuisines: Italian
Address: Sestiere Cannaregio 492
30131 Venezia Italy
Phone: +39 04 15246164

#424
I Tre Mercanti
Cuisines: Desserts, Sandwiches
Address: Sestiere Castello 5364
30122 Venezia Italy
Phone: +39 04 15222901

#425
Da Raffaele
Cuisines: Seafood
Address: San Marco 2347
30124 Venezia Italy
Phone: +39 04 15232317

#426
Artigianato d'Arte
Cuisines: Italian
Address: Calle dei Morti 2251
30135 Venezia Italy
Phone: +39 04 15201802

#427
Ostaria Da Robia
Cuisines: Italian
Address: Cannaregio Fondamenta della
Misericordia 2553
30121 Venezia Italy
Phone: +39 04 15244379

#428
Ristorante Osteria Da Fiore
Cuisines: Pizza
Address: Sestiere Santa Croce 1459
30135 Venezia Italy
Phone: +39 04 15240016

#429
All'armonia
Cuisines: Italian
Address: Sestiere Dorsoduro 924
30123 Venezia Italy
Phone: +39 04 15206895

#430
Cence Fastidis
Cuisines: Italian
Address: Sestiere Dorsoduro 2753A
30123 Venezia Italy
Phone: +39 04 15230531

#431
Osteria al Bomba
Cuisines: Italian
Address: Strada Nuova
30121 Venezia Italy
Phone: +39 04 15205175

#432
Al Murazzi
Cuisines: Italian
Address: Via dei Kirchmayr 16
30100 Venezia Italy
Phone: +39 04 15267278

#433
Real
Cuisines: Italian
Address: Sestiere Castello 4535
30122 Venezia Italy
Phone: +39 04 15211213

#434
Cantina DA Fior
Cuisines: Italian
Address: Via Sestiere Santa Croce 644B
30135 Venezia Italy
Phone: +39 04 15244359

#435
Tiziano
Cuisines: Fast Food
Address: Sestiere Cannaregio, 5747
30131 Venezia Italy
Phone: +39 04 15235544

#436
Macelleria Bergamo di Bergamo Daniela SNC / Daniela
Cuisines: Deli
Address: Via Cannareggio, 1415
30121 Venezia Italy
Phone: +39 04 1715214

#437
Sartori Cicogna Maria
Cuisines: Deli
Address: Via Pescaria 5A
30126 Venezia Italy
Phone: +39 04 1770609

#438
Trattoria Bertolini Maria Luisa
Cuisines: Italian
Address: Sestiere Cannaregio 652
30131 Venezia Italy
Phone: +39 04 1720211

#439
Cip's Club Del Palazzetto
Cuisines: Italian
Address: Isola Isola Della Giudecca 10
30135 Venezia Italy
Phone: +39 04 12408575

#440
Piccolo Martini
Cuisines: Italian
Address: Sestiere San Marco 1501
30124 Venezia Italy
Phone: +39 04 15285136

#441
Canova
Cuisines: Italian
Address: San Marco 1243
30124 Venezia Italy
Phone: +39 04 15289840

#442
San Stefano
Cuisines: Italian
Address: Via San Marco 2776
30124 Venezia Italy
Phone: +39 390 415232467

#443
Le Bistrot de Venise
Cuisines: Beer, Wine & Spirits, Venetian
Address: Calle dei Fabbri 4685
30124 Venice Italy
Phone: +39 04 15236651

#444
Trattoria AL Vagon
Cuisines: Bistro
Address: Sestiere Cannaregio
30131 Venezia Italy
Phone: +39 04 15237558

#445
Al Bucaniere
Cuisines: Pizza
Address: Strada Casa Rossa 22
30100 Venezia Italy
Phone: +39 04 1731156

#446
BON Massimo e Pinzan Paolo
Cuisines: Deli
Address: Sestiere S. Martino Destra, 443
30012 Venezia Italy
Phone: +39 04 1730056

#447
Zane Marco & Rossi Daniela
Cuisines: Deli
Address: Sestiere S. Martino Destra, 71
30012 Venezia Italy
Phone: +39 04 1730214

#448
Osteria AL Ponte del Diavolo
Cuisines: Italian
Address: Isola Torcello 10
30100 Venezia Italy
Phone: +39 04 1730401

#449
Trattoria Da Nino
Cuisines: Gluten-Free, Pizza, Seafood
Address: Sestiere Castello 4668
30122 Venezia Italy
Phone: +39 04 15235886

#450
Trattoria DA Rino
Cuisines: Italian
Address: Sestiere Cannaregio 5642
30121 Venezia Italy
Phone: +39 04 15206998

#451
Osteria Trefanti
Cuisines: Seafood, Venetian
Address: Rio Marin 888
30135 Venezia Italy
Phone: +39 04 15201789

#452
Pizzeria Al Profeta
Cuisines: Pizza
Address: Dorsoduro 2671
30122 Lido di Venezia Italy
Phone: +39 04 15237466

#453
Pizzeria Trattoria 'dai Tosi'
Cuisines: Pizza
Address: Sestiere Castello, 738
30100 Venezia Italy
Phone: +39 04 15237016

#454
Trattoria AL Ponte di Borgo
Cuisines: Bistro
Address: Calle Mercerie,
30100 Venezia Italy
Phone: +39 04 1770090

#455
Osteria da Toni
Cuisines: Italian
Address: Fondamente San Basilio 1642
30123 Venezia Italy
Phone: +39 04 15238272

#456
Omnibus
Cuisines: Fast Food
Address: Strada San Marco 4171
30124 Venezia Italy
Phone: +39 04 15237213

#457
Alla Borsa
Cuisines: Italian
Address: Calle Delle Veste
30124 Venezia Italy
Phone: +39 04 15235434

#458
**Societa' Industrie Alimentari
Ristorazione Collettiva**
Cuisines: Italian
Address: Loc. SAN Pietro IN Volta 322H
30100 Venezia Italy
Phone: +39 04 15279020

#459
Capitan Uncino - Taverna
Cuisines: Italian
Address: Sestiere S. Croce 1501
30135 Venezia Italy
Phone: +39 04 1721901

#460
BAR Oasi di Jiang G
Cuisines: Pizza
Address: Via SAN Marco Calle dei Fabbri,
920 30124 Venezia Italy
Phone: +39 04 15285598

#461
Da Gianni
Cuisines: Italian
Address: Sestiere Cannaregio 4325
30121 Venezia Italy
Phone: +39 04 15287891

#462
La Bella Pollastrella
Cuisines: Italian
Address: Sestiere Cannaregio 408
30131 Venezia Italy
Phone: +39 04 15227613

#463
Pizzeria Ae Oche
Cuisines: Pizza
Address: Sestiere Santa Croce 1552
30135 Venezia Italy
Phone: +39 04 15241161

#464
Trattoria Canonica
Cuisines: Italian, Pizza
Address: Calle Canonica 340
30124 Venezia Italy
Phone: +39 04 15225365

#465
**Ri.al. di Enzo Paolino
e Fagnilli Antonino Bruno**
Cuisines: Pizza
Address: Sestiere Dorsoduro, 1309
30123 Venezia Italy
Phone: +39 04 15236518

#466
Locanda Cipriani
Cuisines: Italian
Address: Piazza Santa Fosca 29
30142 Venezia Italy
Phone: +39 04 1730150

#467
Al Vecio Marangon
Cuisines: Venetian
Address: Campiello Centro Pietro
30123 VE Italy
Phone: +39 04 15235768

#468
Pizza Pause Lory
Cuisines: Pizza
Address: Strada Cannaregio 5608
30131 Venezia Italy
Phone: +39 04 12770065

#469 ,
Trattoria Pizzeria DA Gioia
Cuisines: Pizza, Italian
Address: Sestiere S. Marco, 1016
30124 Venezia Italy
Phone: +39 04 15223649

#470
Philadelphia
Cuisines: Italian
Address: Sestiere Santa Croce 278
30135 Venezia Italy
Phone: +39 04 1711007

#471
Pizzeria Bar ai Tre Archi
Cuisines: Pizza, Seafood
Address: Cannaregio 552
30121 Venezia Italy
Phone: +39 04 1716438

#472
Gaetani / Ermes
Cuisines: Deli
Address: Sestiere Cannaregio, 1331
30121 Venezia Italy
Phone: +39 04 1717402

#473
Trattoria Da Bepi
Cuisines: Italian
Address: Sestiere Cannaregio 4550
30121 Venezia Italy
Phone: +39 04 15285031

#474
Le Fondamenta
Cuisines: Italian
Address: Sestiere Cannaregio 2578
30121 Venezia Italy
Phone: +39 04 15289020

#475
Pizza 2000
Cuisines: Pizza
Address: Rio Terrà Secondo, 2287
30125 Venezia Italy
Phone: +44 4171 3250

#476
Costantini Diego
Cuisines: Pizza
Address: Fondamenta Dei Vetrai 53
30141 Venezia Italy
Phone: +39 04 1739131

#477
Al Parlamento
Cuisines: Italian
Address: Fondamenta San Giobbe 511
30121 Venezia Italy
Phone: +39 04 12440214

#478
Taverna San Lio
Cuisines: Italian
Address: Calle del Cafetier 5562
30100 Venezia Italy
Phone: +39 04 12770669

#479
Al Vecio Portal
Cuisines: Italian
Address: Campiello Dello Pescheria
30122 VE Italy
Phone: +39 04 15287765

#480
Osteria al Bacareto
Cuisines: Bar, Italian
Address: 3447 San Samuele
30124 Venezia Italy
Phone: +39 04 15289336

#481
San Giorgio
Cuisines: Italian
Address: Sestiere Castello
30122 Venezia Italy
Phone: +39 04 15231993

#482
Trattoria al Ponte
Cuisines: Italian
Address: Santa Croce 1666
30135 Venezia Italy
Phone: +39 04 1719777

#483
Alberghi: Ca' Pisani
Cuisines: Italian
Address: Sestiere Dorsoduro 979
30123 Venezia Italy
Phone: +39 04 12401411

#484
Ai Mercanti
Cuisines: Italian
Address: Calle dei Fuseri Corte Coppo
4346A 30124 San Marco Italy
Phone: +39 04 15238269

#485
Q Food & More
Cuisines: Pizza, Cupcakes, Sandwiches
Address: San Marco 5464
30124 Venezia Italy
Phone: +39 04 12960057

#486
Still Novo
Cuisines: Italian
Address: Via San Marco 1659B
30124 Venezia Italy
Phone: +39 04 12960664

#487
Sansovino
Cuisines: Italian
Address: San Marco 2628 Venezia Italy
Phone: +39 415 286141

#488
Bar Novo
Cuisines: Italian
Address: San Marco 5456
30124 Venezia Italy
Phone: +39 04 12777965

#489
**Osteria La Bottega
ai Promessi Sposi**
Cuisines: Italian
Address: Calle Dell'Oca 4367
30121 Venice Italy
Phone: +39 04 12412747

#490
Al Prosecco
Cuisines: Italian, Caterers
Address: S.re Santa Croce 1503
30135 Venezia Italy
Phone: +39 04 15240222

#491
Carpaccio
Cuisines: Italian
Address: Castello 4088
30122 VE Italy
Phone: +39 04 1528916

#492
Alla Vecchia Fornace
Cuisines: Venetian
Address: Fdm Dei Vetrai 35
30141 Murano Italy
Phone: +39 04 15274244

#493
Trattoria CEA
Cuisines: Italian
Address: Sestiere Cannaregio 5422
30121 Venezia Italy
Phone: +39 04 15237450

#494
Planet
Cuisines: Italian, Pizza, Seafood
Address: Calle de La Caselleria 5281
30122 VE Italy
Phone: +39 04 15220808

#495
Hostaria Da Franz
Cuisines: Italian
Address: Salizada San Antonin 3499
30122 VE Italy
Phone: +39 00 390415220861

#496
Majer Cafe Bakery
Cuisines: Cafe, Bakeries, Coffee & Tea
Address: Santa Croce 1630
30015 Chioggia Italy
Phone: +39 04 1710385

#497
Restaurant AL Peloceto Risorto
Cuisines: Italian
Address: Via San Polo 249
30125 Venezia Italy
Phone: +39 04 15225953

#498
Al Vecio Penasa Birreria
Cuisines: Bistro, Dive Bar
Address: Sestiere Castello 4585
30122 Venezia Italy
Phone: +39 04 15237202

#499
Il Ridotto
Cuisines: Italian
Address: Castello 4509
30122 Venezia Italy
Phone: +39 04 15208280

#500
Tian Jin
Cuisines: Chinese
Address: Sestiere San Polo 649
30125 Venezia Italy
Phone: +39 04 15204603

TOP 300 ATTRACTIONS
The Most Recommended by Locals & Trevelers
(From #1 to #300)

#1
Palazzo Ducale
Category: Museum
Address: Piazza San Marco 1
30124 Venezia Italy
Phone: +39 04 12715911

#2
Ente per La Conservazione Della Gondola
Category: Leisure Center
Address: Sestiere SAN Marco, 3613
30124 Venezia Italy
Phone: +39 04 15211534

#3
Piazza San Marco
Category: Landmark, Historical Buildings
Address: Piazza San Marco
30124 Venezia Italy
Phone: +39 04 17241040

#4
Peggy Guggenheim Collection
Category: Landmark,
Historical Buildings, Museum
Address: Dorsoduro 704
30100 Venezia Italy
Phone: +39 04 12405411

#5
Venezia Turismo Consorzio Motoscafi
Category: Boating
Address: Isola Nova del Tronchetto, 24/A
30100 Venezia Italy
Phone: +39 04 15209762

#6
Teatro La Fenice
Category: Performing Arts, Landmark,
Historical Buildings
Address: Campo San Fantin 1965
30124 Venezia Italy
Phone: +39 04 1786511

#7
Basilica di San Marco
Category: Landmark,
Historical Buildings, Cemetery
Address: Piazza San Marco
30124 Venezia Italy
Phone: +39 04 12404311

#8
Gallerie dell Accademia di Venezia
Category: Landmark,
Historical Buildings, Museum
Address: Campo della Carità 1050
30123 Venezia Italy

#9
Taverna del Campiello Remer
Category: Jazz & Blues
Address: Cannaregio 5701
30125 Venezia Italy
Phone: +39 04 15228789

#10
Musée Ca' d'Oro
Category: Landmark, Historical Buildings,
Museum
Address: calle di Ca' d'Oro 3932
30121 Venezia Italy
Phone: +39 04 15278790

#11
Ponte dell'Accademia
Category: Lake
Address: Venezia Italy

#12
Santa Maria Gloriosa dei Frari
Category: Landmark, Historical Buildings,
Religious Organization
Address: Campo dei Frari
30125 Venezia Italy

#13
Ghetto de Venise
Category: Cultural Center, Landmark,
Historical Buildings
Address: Ghetto Vecchio
30121 Venezia Italy

#14
Societa': Serenissima Motoscafi
Category: Boating
Address: Sestiere Castello, 4545
30122 Venezia Italy
Phone: +39 04 15224281

#15
Le Grand Canal
Category: Landmark, Historical Buildings
Address: Venezia Italy
Phone: +39 04 15200501

#16
Scuola Grande di San Rocco
Category: Museum
Address: Salizzada San Rocco
30124 Venezia Italy

#17
Archeoclub D'italia
Sede di Venezia
Category: Leisure Center
Address: Sestiere Cannaregio, 1376/A
30121 Venezia Italy
Phone: +39 04 1710515

#18
Carnevale
Category: Performing Arts, Museum
Address: Piazza San Marco
30124 Venezia Italy
Phone: +39 04 12702411

#19
Parco San Giuliano
Category: Park
Address: Mestre, Venezia Italy

#20
Libreria Acqua Alta
di Frizzo Luigi
Category: Bookstores, Landmark,
Historical Buildings
Address: Sestiere Castello 5167
30122 Venezia Italy
Phone: +39 04 12960841

#21
Musei Civici Museo Vetrario
Category: Museum
Address: Fondamenta Giustinian Marco 8
30141 Venezia Italy
Phone: +39 04 1739586

#22
Fondazione UGO e Olga Levi
Category: Leisure Center
Address: Sestiere S. Marco, 2893
30124 Venezia Italy
Phone: +39 04 1786777

#23
Ponte dei Sospiri
Category: Landmark, Historical Buildings
Address: Riva dei Schiavoni
30123 Venezia Italy

#24
Galleria Ca' Rezzonico
Category: Art Gallery
Address: Via Sestiere Di Dorsoduro 2793
30123 Venezia Italy
Phone: +39 04 15280035

#25
Associazione Body World
Category: Sports Club
Address: Sestiere S. Croce, 2196/A
30100 Venezia Italy
Phone: +39 04 1710657

#26
île Burano
Category: Landmark,
Historical Buildings, Hotels & Travel
Address: Venezia Italy

#27
Palazzo Grassi
Category: Art Gallery
Address: 3231 Campo San Samuele
30124 Venezia Italy
Phone: +39 04 15236180

#28
Venetian Heritage
Category: Leisure Center
Address: Sestiere S. Marco, 3366
30124 Venezia Italy
Phone: +39 04 12770780

#29
Santa Maria della Salute
Category: Landmark, Historical Buildings,
Religious Organization
Address: Campo Salute
30100 Venezia Italy
Phone: +39 04 12743911

#30
Museo Storico Navale di Venezia
Category: Museum
Address: Riva San Biasio Castello 2148
30122 Venezia Italy
Phone: +39 04 12441399

#31
Agenzia Nautica
Base Mare 21 S.N
Category: Boating
Address: Sestiere Dorsoduro, 1316/A
30123 Venezia Italy
Phone: +39 04 15210740

#32
La Torre dellorologio
Category: Landmark, Historical Buildings
Address: Piazza San Marco
30124 Venezia Italy

#33
Basilica di Santa Maria
Category: Basilica
Address: Sestiere Dorsoduro
30123 Venezia Italy

#34
CUS Venezia
Category: Fitness & Instruction
Address: Sestiere Dorsoduro, 2407
30123 Venezia Italy
Phone: +39 04 15246619

#35
Murano Venetian Glass Center
Category: Art Gallery
Address: Calle San Cipriano 48
30100 Venezia Italy
Phone: +39 04 1736894

#36
Istituto Veneziano per La Storia Della Resistenza
Category: Leisure Center
Address: Sestiere Dorsoduro, 54
30123 Venezia Italy
Phone: +39 04 15287735

#37
Basilique San Giovanni
Category: Landmark, Historical Buildings, Religious Organization
Address: Santi dei Giovanni e Paolo
30122 Venezia Italy
Phone: +39 04 15237510

#38
Teatro Malibran
Category: Performing Arts, Landmark, Historical Buildings
Address: Venezia Italy

#39
Venice International Foundation
Category: Leisure Center
Address: Sestiere Dorsoduro, 3144
30123 Venezia Italy
Phone: +39 04 12770608

#40
Monumento a Daniele Manin
Category: Landmark, Historical Buildings
Address: Venezia Italy

#41
Teatro San Gallo
Category: Performing Arts
Address: Calle Cavalletto
30124 Venezia Italy
Phone: +39 04 12412002

#42
Giovane Montagna
Category: Sports Club
Address: Sestiere Dorsoduro, 3703
30123 Venezia Italy
Phone: +39 04 15229235

#43
Markusdom
Category: Landmark, Historical Buildings, Religious Organization
Address: Piazza San Marco
30124 Venezia Italy
Phone: +39 415 224064

#44
La Biennale
Category: Landmark, Historical Buildings
Address: Sestiere Castello
30122 Venezia Italy
Phone: +39 04 15238159

#45
Scuola Grande Carmini
Category: Museum, Leisure Center
Address: Sestiere Dorsoduro, 2617
30123 Venezia Italy
Phone: +39 04 15289420

#46
Ca' Pesaro International Gallery of Modern Art and Museum of
Category: Art Gallery
Address: 2077
30135 Venezia Italy

#47
ESU di Venezia
Category: Leisure Center
Address: Sestiere Dorsoduro, 3861
30123 Venezia Italy
Phone: +39 04 1714415

#48
Statue du Condottiere Bartoloméo Colleoni
Category: Landmark, Historical Buildings
Address: Santi dei Giovanni e Paolo
30122 Venezia Italy

#49
L'Isola
Category: Flowers & Gifts, Art Gallery
Address: Sestiere San Marco 1468
30124 Venezia Italy
Phone: +39 04 15231973

#50
Circolo Societa' Dell'unione
Category: Leisure Center
Address: Sestiere Dorsoduro, 878
30123 Venezia Italy
Phone: +39 04 15225005

#51
Scala Contarini
Category: Landmark, Historical Buildings
Address: Corte Contarini 4306
30124 Venezia Italy

#52
Musei Civici - Palazzo Mocenigo Storia del Tessuto e Costume
Category: Museum
Address: Sestiere S. Croce, 1992
30135 Venezia Italy
Phone: +39 04 1721798

#53
Fondazione Studium Generale Marcianum per La Promozione di
Category: Leisure Center
Address: Sestiere Dorsoduro,
30123 Venezia Italy
Phone: +39 04 12743911

#54
Santa Maria della Pièta
Category: Landmark, Historical Buildings
Address: Riva degli Schiavoni
Venezia Italy

#55
La Bienale
Category: Landmark, Historical Buildings
Address: San Polo 2004
30124 Venezia Italy
Phone: +39 04 12753311

#56
The Emily Harvey Foundation
Category: Leisure Center
Address: Sestiere Dorsoduro, 3521/A
30123 Venezia Italy
Phone: +39 04 15244567

#57
La Scuola Grande San Marco
Category: Landmark, Historical Buildings
Address: Santi dei Giovanni e Paolo
30122 Venezia Italy

#58
Wenecja
Category: Cultural Center
Address: Venezia Italy

#59
Cent.Studi-Docum.Cultura Armena
Category: Leisure Center
Address: Sestiere Dorsoduro, 1602
30123 Venezia Italy
Phone: +39 04 15224225

#60
Ponte Scalzi
Category: Landmark, Historical Buildings
Address: Piazzale Roma Venezia Italy

#61
Galleria San Maurizio
Category: Art Gallery
Address: Sestiere Dorsoduro 195
30123 Venezia Italy
Phone: +39 04 15212510

#62
Compagnia Della Vela
Category: Sports Club
Address: Sestiere Dorsoduro, 260
30123 Venezia Italy
Phone: +39 04 15238268

#63
Le Marché du Rialto
Category: Landmark, Historical Buildings
Address: Arrêt Mercato Venezia Italy

#64
S.Giacomo in Palude
Category: Landmark, Historical Buildings, Arts & Entertainment
Address: Venezia Italy

#65
Consorzio Motoscafi Venezia
Category: Boating
Address: Sestiere Dorsoduro, 167
30123 Venezia Italy
Phone: +39 04 15231031

#66
Sotoportego dei Preti
Category: Landmark, Historical Buildings
Address: Venezia Italy

#67
Ca d'Oro
Category: Museum
Address: Sestiere Cannaregio
30121 Venezia Italy

#68
Associazione Amici Della Fenice
Category: Leisure Center
Address: Sestiere S. Marco, 1897
30124 Venezia Italy
Phone: +39 04 12414182

#69
Ile San Michele
Category: Landmark, Historical Buildings
Address: Venezia Italy

#70
Giudecca Art Gallery 795
Category: Art Gallery
Address: Fondamenta San Biagio 795
Giudecca 30133 Venezia Italy
Phone: +39 04 17241182

#71
Compagnia Della Vela
Category: Sports Club
Address: Sestiere S. Marco, 2
30124 Venezia Italy
Phone: +39 04 15200884

#72
Torcello
Category: Landmark, Historical Buildings
Address: Venezia Italy

#73
Cartoleria Accademia
Category: Museum
Address: Sestiere Dorsoduro, 1007/A
30123 Venezia Italy
Phone: +39 04 15285283

#74
Traghetto Gondole Molo
Category: Boating
Address: Sestiere S. Marco, 1
30124 Venezia Italy
Phone: +39 04 15200685

#75
San Simeone Piccolo
Category: Landmark, Historical Buildings
Address: Santa Croce
30135 Venezia Italy

#76
Isola di San Servolo
Category: Landmark, Historical Buildings,
Arts & Entertainment
Address: Venezia Italy

#77
Associazione Stazio Dogana
Category: Boating
Address: Sestiere S. Marco, 213
30124 Venezia Italy
Phone: +39 04 15206120

#78
Zattere
Category: Landmark, Historical Buildings
Address: Fondamenta delle Zattere
30123 Venezia Italy

#79
Interpreti Veneziani
Category: Music Venues
Address: San Marco 2862B
30124 Venezia Italy
Phone: +39 04 12770561

#80
Alilaguna
Category: Boating
Address: Sestiere S. Marco, 4267/A
30124 Venezia Italy
Phone: +39 04 15235775

#81
Arsenale / Venetian Arsenal
Category: Landmark, Historical Buildings
Address: Riva S. Biasio Castello
30122 Venezia Italy
Phone: +39 394 12441399

#82
Al Paradiso Perduto
Category: Music Venues
Address: Venezia Italy

#83
**Associazione Culturale
le Colonete**
Category: Leisure Center
Address: Sestiere S. Marco, 993
30124 Venezia Italy
Phone: +39 04 15222828

#84
Santa Maria Assunta
Category: Landmark, Historical Buildings,
Religious Organization
Address: Venezia Italy

#85
Novecento
Category: Jazz & Blues
Address: Sestiere San Polo 900
30125 Venezia Italy
Phone: +39 04 15226565

#86
**Centri: Internazionale
Della Grafica**
Category: Leisure Center
Address: Sestiere S. Marco, 3579
30124 Venezia Italy
Phone: +39 04 15221825

#87
Venice Water Fountains
Category: Landmark, Historical Buildings
Address: Venezia Italy

#88
**Peggy Guggenheim eine
Sammlerin...**
Category: Museum
Address: Palazzo Venier dei Leoni
30124 Venezia Italy

#89
**Scuola di Danza
Prof. Marina Prando**
Category: Dance Studio
Address: Sestiere S. Marco, 2507/A
30124 Venezia Italy
Phone: +39 04 15239457

#90
Venise la Sérénissime
Category: Landmark, Historical Buildings
Address: Venezia Italy

#91
**Museo Archeologico
Nazionale di Venezia**
Category: Museum
Address: Piazza San Marco
30124 Venezia Italy

#92
Circoli: del Bridge di Venezia
Category: Leisure Center
Address: Sestiere S. Marco, 4013/A
30124 Venezia Italy
Phone: +39 04 15225337

#93
Geto
Category: Museum
Address: Ponte Guglie
30121 Venezia Italy

#94
Libreria Studium
Category: Library
Address: San Marco 337
30124 Venezia Italy
Phone: +39 04 15222382

#95
Musée Correr
Category: Museum
Address: Venezia Italy
Phone: +39 04 15225625

#96
Traghetto Trinita'
Category: Boating
Address: Sestiere S. Marco, S.N.
30124 Venezia Italy
Phone: +39 04 15231837

#97
San Nicolò dei Mendicoli
Category: Landmark, Historical Buildings
Address: Campo San Nicolò 1907
30100 Venezia Italy

#98
Ateneo di San Basso
Category: Music Venues
Address: Piazza San Marco
30124 Venezia Italy

#99
Universita' Della Terza Eta' del Centro Storico
Category: Leisure Center
Address: Sestiere S. Marco, 4571
30124 Venezia Italy
Phone: +39 04 15225336

#100
Chiesa di San Salvador
Category: Landmark, Historical Buildings
Address: Salizzada di San Salvador
Venezia Italy

#101
Cinema: Multisala Giorgione
Category: Cinema
Address: Via Cannaregio 4612
30121 Venezia Italy
Phone: +39 04 15226298

#102
Traghetto Dogana CA' Vallaresso
Category: Boating
Address: Sestiere S. Marco, 1
30124 Venezia Italy
Phone: +39 04 15239981

#103
L'île San Francesco del Deserto
Category: Landmark, Historical Buildings
Address: Venezia Italy

#104
San Lazzaro degli Armeni
Category: Castle
Address: Isola di San Lazzaro degli Armeni,
30126 Venezia Italy

#105
Associazione Sportiva Federcacciatori Sez. Com. di Venezia
Category: Sports Club
Address: Sestiere S. Marco, 3743/A
30124 Venezia Italy
Phone: +39 04 15239146

#106
Artis Di Lorenzo Usicco
Category: Gallery
Address: S.Croce 1811
30135 Venezia Italy
Phone: +39 04 1710427

#107
Universita' Popolare di Venezia
Category: Leisure Center
Address: Sestiere S. Marco, 52
30124 Venezia Italy
Phone: +39 04 15287544

#108
Palazzo Dario
Category: Landmark, Historical Buildings
Address: am Canal Grande
30100 Venezia Italy

#109
Teatro Goldoni
Category: Performing Arts
Address: Piazza Piazza San Marco 46
30034 Venezia Italy
Phone: +39 04 12402014

#110
Associazione Maria Callas
Category: Leisure Center
Address: Sestiere S. Marco, 2919
30124 Venezia Italy
Phone: +39 04 12410828

#111
Musica A Palazzo
Category: Opera
Address: Sottoportego Barbarigo 2504-
2506/A 30124 Venezia Italy

#112
Circoli: Artistico
Category: Leisure Center
Address: Sestiere S. Marco, 4209
30124 Venezia Italy
Phone: +39 04 15225707

#113
Tour de l'horloge
Category: Landmark, Historical Buildings
Address: Place Saint Marc
30124 Venezia Italy

#114
Osteria Blues Bar All'alba
Category: Jazz & Blues
Address: Sestiere San Marco 5370
30125 Venezia Italy

#115
Unione per Lo Sviluppo dei Valori Morali Sezione
Category: Leisure Center
Address: Sestiere S. Marco, 1513
30124 Venezia Italy
Phone: +39 04 15222796

#116
Palazzo Memmo Martinengo-Mandelli
Category: Landmark, Historical Buildings
Address: Cannareggio 1756
30121 Venezia Italy

#117
Teatro Fondamenta Nuove
Category: Performing Arts
Address: Via Cannaregio 5013
30121 Venezia Italy
Phone: +39 04 15224498

#118
Cultura Venezia Futura
Category: Leisure Center
Address: Sestiere S. Marco, 2893
30124 Venezia Italy
Phone: +39 04 12770542

#119
Biblioteca Nazionale Marciana
Category: Museum, Library
Address: Sestiere S. Marco, 7
30124 Venezia Italy
Phone: +39 04 12407211

#120
Palazzo Fortuny
Category: Museum
Address: Campo san Beneto
30124 Venezia Italy
Phone: +39 04 12747607

#121
Venezia Iniziative Culturali
Category: Leisure Center
Address: Sestiere S. Marco, 2847
30124 Venezia Italy
Phone: +39 04 15204372

#122
Campanile di San Marco
Category: Landmark, Historical Buildings
Address: Piazza San Marco 30124
30124 Venezia Italy
Phone: +39 04 12708311

#123
Centro Teatrale di Ricerca
Category: Leisure Center
Address: Calle DE La Madonna
Giudecca, 621 30142 Venezia Italy
Phone: +39 04 15231039

#124
Università Ca' Foscari
Category: Library, University
Address: Calle Cereria Dorsoduro
30121 Venezia Italy

#125
Palazzo Pisani moretta
Category: Castle
Address: Venezia Italy

#126
Fondazione Castelforte
Category: Leisure Center
Address: Via S.polo, 3106
30125 Venezia Italy
Phone: +39 04 12759399

#127
Campo dei Gesuiti
Category: Landmark, Historical Buildings
Address: Venezia Italy

#128
Cà Zanardi
Category: Castle
Address: Venezia Italy

#129
A. Rubelli
Category: Boating
Address: Via SAN Polo, 432
30100 Venezia Italy
Phone: +39 04 15229521

#130
Express Shipping CO.
Category: Couriers & Delivery Services
Address: Sestiere S. Marco, 4467
30124 Venezia Italy
Phone: +39 04 15206800

#131
Teatro La Fenice
Category: Performing Arts
Address: Localita' Campo S.
Fantin Venezia Italy
Phone: +39 04 12424

#132
CA' Zanardi
Category: Leisure Center
Address: Via Cannaregio, 4132
30121 Venezia Italy
Phone: +39 04 12410220

#133
Centro di Studi Teologici G.
Category: Library
Address: Sestiere S. Marco, 2760
30124 Venezia Italy
Phone: +39 04 15238673

#134
Biennale Di Venezia Giardini
Category: Art Gallery
Address: Calle Paludo
30122 Venezia Italy
Phone: +39 04 15218711

#135
Associazione Culturale Italo Tedesca
Category: Leisure Center
Address: Via Cannaregio, 4118
30121 Venezia Italy
Phone: +39 04 15245275

#136
Scuola Dalmata dei SS Giorgio e Trifone
Category: Library
Address: Sestiere Castello, 3297
30122 Venezia Italy
Phone: +39 04 15208446

#137
Viani Nadia
Category: Art Gallery
Address: Via Dorsoduro, 1195
30123 Venezia Italy
Phone: +39 04 15223159

#138
Associazione Rialto MIO
Category: Leisure Center
Address: Sestiere SAN Polo, 2516
30125 Venezia Italy
Phone: +39 04 1715931

#139
Murano Island
Category: Landmark, Historical Buildings
Address: Piazzale Calle Colonna
30141 Murano Italy

#140
Teatro Piccolo Arsenale
Category: Performing Arts
Address: Campiello Tana
30122 Venezia Italy
Phone: +39 04 15218898

#141
Piccola Soc. Coop.Taxi Boat Services A RI
Category: Boating
Address: Sestiere SAN Polo, 1151
30125 Venezia Italy
Phone: +39 04 12960570

#142
Museo Archeologico
Category: Museum
Address: Sestiere S. Marco, 17
30124 Venezia Italy
Phone: +39 04 15225978

#143
FAI Fondo per L'ambiente Italiano
Category: Leisure Center
Address: Sestiere SAN Polo, 2025
30125 Venezia Italy
Phone: +39 04 1719707

#144
Teatro Alle Tese
Category: Performing Arts
Address: Calle della Tana 2169
30122 Venezia Italy

#145
Associazione Culturale Proposta per Venezia
Category: Leisure Center
Address: Sestiere SAN Polo, 2171
30125 Venezia Italy
Phone: +39 04 1713490

#146
Itaca Art Studio di Martin Monica
Category: Art Gallery
Address: Sestiere Castello 5267A
30122 Venezia Italy
Phone: +39 04 15203207

#147
**Associazione Culturale
di Danza e Teatro Kairs**
Category: Leisure Center
Address: Sestiere SAN Polo, 3105
30125 Venezia Italy
Phone: +39 04 15243783

#148
Museo Correr
Category: Museum
Address: Piazza San Marco 52
30124 Venezia Italy
Phone: +39 04 12405211

#149
Traghetto S. Toma'
Category: Boating
Address: Sestiere SAN Polo, 2812
30125 Venezia Italy
Phone: +39 04 15205275

#150
Casino' Municipale di Venezia
Category: Casino
Address: Sestiere Cannaregio 2040
30121 Venezia Italy
Phone: +39 04 15297111

#151
Cooperative: Scalo Fluviale
Category: Boating
Address: Isola Nova del Tronchetto, 500
30100 Venezia Italy
Phone: +39 04 15222391

#152
**Musei Civici
Museo di Storia Naturale**
Category: Museum
Address: Sestiere San Croce 1730
30135 Venezia Italy
Phone: +39 04 12750206

#153
Ducale
Category: Boating
Address: Isola Nova del Tronchetto, 23
30100 Venezia Italy
Phone: +39 04 15227255

#154
Musei Civico
Category: Museum
Address: Sestiere Dorsoduro 3136
30123 Venezia Italy
Phone: +39 04 12410100

#155
Unione Sportiva Alvisiana
Category: Sports Club
Address: Via Cannaregio, 31/44
30100 Venezia Italy
Phone: +39 04 15240920

#156
**Vetreria Artistica
Archimede Seguso**
Category: Museum
Address: Fondamenta Serenella 18
30141 Venezia Italy
Phone: +39 04 1739065

#157
Unione Sportiva Alvisiana
Category: Sports Club
Address: Via Cannareggio, 32
30100 Venezia Italy
Phone: +39 04 1716543

#158
**Giovanni Maria Fiore
Editore D'arte**
Category: Art Gallery
Address: Via CA' Savorgnan, 12
30172 Venezia Italy
Phone: +39 04 1957194

#159
**Istituto Veneto
per I Beni Culturali**
Category: Leisure Center
Address: Sestiere Castello, 4856
30122 Venezia Italy
Phone: +39 04 15285585

#160
Parrocchia S. Cassiano
Category: Museum
Address: Sestiere SAN Polo, 1852
30125 Venezia Italy
Phone: +39 04 1721408

#161
Clubneroverde Alla Vigna Associazione
Category: Sports Club
Address: Via Castello, 3163
30122 Venezia Italy
Phone: +39 04 15224570

#162
Barovier Marino
Category: Art Gallery
Address: Sestiere S. Marco, 3202
30124 Venezia Italy
Phone: +39 04 15236748

#163
Marazzi / Loris
Category: Art Gallery
Address: Sestiere Dorsoduro, 369
30123 Venezia Italy
Phone: +39 04 15239001

#164
SAN Salvador
Category: Boating
Address: Sestiere Castello, 3814
30122 Venezia Italy
Phone: +39 04 15224222

#165
Soprintendenza per I Beni Artistici e Storici di Venezia
Category: Museum
Address: Sestiere Cannaregio, 3932
30131 Venezia Italy
Phone: +39 04 15222349

#166
Associazioni: Nazionale Combattenti e Reduci
Category: Leisure Center
Address: Sestiere Castello, 5016/B
30122 Venezia Italy
Phone: +39 04 15220630

#167
Galleria D' Arte Contini
Category: Art Gallery
Address: Via Giorgio Ferro, 11
30174 Venezia Italy
Phone: +39 04 1980863

#168
Gruppo Anziani Autogestiti
Category: Leisure Center
Address: Sestiere Castello, 5065/I
30122 Venezia Italy
Phone: +39 04 15222779

#169
Gruppo Furlan Cinecity di G.
Category: Cinema
Address: Via Premuda,
30171 Venezia Italy
Phone: +39 04 1989101

#170
A.S.D. NV Serenissima
Category: Sports Club
Address: Sestiere Castello, 2752
30122 Venezia Italy
Phone: +39 04 12960624

#171
Gruppo Furlan Cinecity di G.
Category: Cinema
Address: Via Palazzo, 29
30174 Venezia Italy
Phone: +39 04 1954486

#172
Unione Sportiva Remiera Francescana
Category: Sports Club
Address: Sestiere Castello, 2737
30122 Venezia Italy
Phone: +39 04 15229527

#173
Scuola Grande di San Giovanni Evangelista
Category: Museum
Address: Sestiere SAN Polo, 2454
30125 Venezia Italy
Phone: +39 04 1718234

#174
Fondazione Giorgio Cini
Category: Leisure Center
Address: Isola S. Giorgio Maggiore, S.N.
30124 Venezia Italy
Phone: +39 04 12710211

#175
**Arciconfraternita Scuola
Grande di S. Rocco**
Category: Museum
Address: Sestiere SAN Polo, 3064
30125 Venezia Italy
Phone: +39 04 15242820

#176
Compagnia Della Vela
Category: Sports Club
Address: Isola S. Giorgio Maggiore, SNC
30124 Venezia Italy
Phone: +39 04 15210723

#177
**Arciconfraternita Scuola
Grande di S. Rocco**
Category: Museum
Address: Sestiere SAN Polo, 3054
30125 Venezia Italy
Phone: +39 04 15234864

#178
**Accademia Musicale
di San Giorgio**
Category: Sports Club
Address: Isola S. Giorgio Maggiore, S.N.
30124 Venezia Italy
Phone: +39 04 12771267

#179
**B. & B. ART
di Bugno Massimiliano**
Category: Art Gallery
Address: Sestiere S. Marco, 1996
30124 Venezia Italy
Phone: +39 04 15230360

#180
**Ass. Sportiva Dilettantistica
Proyecto di Vianello**
Category: Dance Studio
Address: Via Sestiere Santa Croce, 1270/B
30135 Venezia Italy
Phone: +39 04 15240707

#181
Galleria Luce Arte Moderna
Category: Art Gallery
Address: Sestiere S. Marco, 1922/A
30124 Venezia Italy
Phone: +39 04 15222949

#182
Narduzzi & Solemar
Category: Boating
Address: Sestiere Castello, 71
30122 Venezia Italy
Phone: +39 04 15231835

#183
Galleria D'arte L'occhio
Category: Art Gallery
Address: Sestiere Dorsoduro, 181
30123 Venezia Italy
Phone: +39 04 15226550

#184
Palestra Athena
Category: Fitness & Instruction
Address: Sestiere Castello, 1017
30122 Venezia Italy
Phone: +39 04 15232203

#185
Zenith
Category: Art Gallery
Address: SRE SAN Marco, 2671
30124 Venezia Italy
Phone: +39 04 15207859

#186
Gruppo Podistico Odeon
Category: Sports Club
Address: Sestiere Castello, 1257
30122 Venezia Italy
Phone: +39 04 12770765

#187
Il Gobbo di Rialto
Category: Arts & Entertainment
Address: Campo San Giacomo di Rialto
30100 Venezia Italy

#188
Anffas di Venezia Onlus
Category: Leisure Center
Address: Sestiere Castello, 1
30122 Venezia Italy
Phone: +39 04 15228758

#189
**Teatro Stabile del Veneto
Carlo Goldoni**
Category: Opera & Ballet, Music Venues
Address: Sestiere S. Marco, 4650
30124 Venezia Italy
Phone: +39 04 12402011

#190
Associazione Venezia & Venice
Category: Leisure Center
Address: Sestiere S. Croce, 1897
30135 Venezia Italy
Phone: +39 04 12759010

#191
Alice in The Wonderland
Category: Art Gallery
Address: Via Castello, 1639
30122 Venezia Italy
Phone: +39 04 15287616

#192
**Associazione Amici dei Musei
e Monumenti Veneziani**
Category: Leisure Center
Address: Sestiere S. Croce, 1992
30135 Venezia Italy
Phone: +39 04 15242552

#193
Galleria Traghetto
Category: Art Gallery
Address: Sestiere S. Marco, 2543
30124 Venezia Italy
Phone: +39 04 15221188

#194
**Deputazione di Storia Patria
per Le Venezie**
Category: Leisure Center
Address: Sestiere S. Croce, 1583
30135 Venezia Italy
Phone: +39 04 15241009

#195
**Padri Domenicani
Convento Ss.giovanni**
Category: Museum, Church
Address: Sestiere Castello, 6363
30122 Venezia Italy
Phone: +39 04 15235913

#196
**Istituto Veneto
per I Beni Culturali**
Category: Leisure Center
Address: SRE SAN Polo, 2454/A
30125 Venezia Italy
Phone: +39 04 1714603

#197
**Soprintendenza per I Beni Artistici
e Storici di Venezia**
Category: Museum
Address: Sestiere Dorsoduro, 170
30123 Venezia Italy
Phone: +39 04 15235971

#198
Tara
Category: Leisure Center
Address: Sestiere S. Croce, 737/A
30135 Venezia Italy
Phone: +39 04 1715311

#199
Studio Arga di Gabriella Tallon
Category: Art Gallery
Address: Sestiere S. Marco, 3659/A
30124 Venezia Italy
Phone: +39 04 12411124

#200
Tappezzeria Nautica Hydromrò
Category: Boating
Address: Giudecca 212C
30133 Venezia Italy
Phone: +39 00 390412770415

#201
Museo di Torcello
Category: Museum
Address: Isola Torcello, 20
30100 Venezia Italy
Phone: +39 04 1730761

#202
Teatrino Della Murata del TPM
Category: Opera & Ballet
Address: Via Giordano Bruno, 19
30174 Venezia Italy
Phone: +39 04 1989879

#203
Ass. Culturale Vortice
Category: Opera & Ballet
Address: Sestiere Cannaregio, 5013
30131 Venezia Italy
Phone: +39 04 12412156

#204
Club Alpino Italiano
Category: Sports Club
Address: Sestiere Cannaregio, 883
30121 Venezia Italy
Phone: +39 04 1716900

#205
**Bressanello ART Studio
di Bressanello Fabio**
Category: Art Gallery
Address: Sestiere Dorsoduro, 2835/A
30123 Venezia Italy
Phone: +39 04 17241080

#206
**Associazioni: Remiera Canottieri
Cannaregio**
Category: Sports Club
Address: Sestiere Cannaregio, 3161
30121 Venezia Italy
Phone: +39 04 1720539

#207
**Fondazione Scientifica
Querini Stampalia**
Category: Museum
Address: Sestiere Castello 4778
30122 Venezia Italy
Phone: +39 04 12711411

#208
**Venice Canoe e Dragon Boat
Associazione Sportiva
Dilettantistica**
Category: Sports Club
Address: Sestiere Cannaregio, 3163
30121 Venezia Italy
Phone: +39 04 1722783

#209
Galleria Il Capricorno
Category: Art Gallery
Address: Sestiere San Marco 1994
30124 Venezia Italy
Phone: +39 04 15206920

#210
Bocciofila S.alvise
Category: Sports Club
Address: Sestiere Cannaregio, 3163
30121 Venezia Italy
Phone: +39 04 12750457

#211
Galleria Daniele Luchetta
Category: Art Gallery
Address: Sestiere San Marco 2513A
30124 Venezia Italy
Phone: +39 04 15285092

#212
Polisportiva San Girolamo
Category: Sports Club
Address: Sestiere Cannaregio, 3006
30131 Venezia Italy
Phone: +39 04 15240339

#213
Galleria D'arte Contini
Category: Art Gallery
Address: Sestiere San Marco 2765
30124 Venezia Italy
Phone: +39 04 15208381

#214
**Associazione Remiera
Punta S.Giobbe**
Category: Sports Club
Address: Sestiere Cannaregio, 3161
30121 Venezia Italy
Phone: +39 04 12757017

#215
Melori & Rosenberg
Category: Art Gallery
Address: Sestiere Di San Polo 2815
30125 Venezia Italy
Phone: +39 04 12750025

#216
Venice Gospel Ensemble
Category: Leisure Center
Address: Sestiere Cannaregio, 1076/B
30121 Venezia Italy
Phone: +39 04 12750531

#217
Novello Michele
Category: Art Gallery
Address: Sestiere San Marco 2016 A
30124 Venezia Italy
Phone: +39 04 15285599

#218
**Circolo Ricreativo Culturale Anziani
di Cannaregio**
Category: Leisure Center
Address: Sestiere Cannaregio, 3152
30121 Venezia Italy
Phone: +39 04 1719393

#219
Soprintendenza Beni Ambientali ED Architettonici del Veneto
Category: Museum, Opera & Ballet
Address: Sestiere S. Croce, 770
30135 Venezia Italy
Phone: +39 04 12574011

#220
Veneziana Motoscafi Gran Turismo
Category: Boating
Address: Sestiere S. Croce, 504
30135 Venezia Italy
Phone: +39 04 1716949

#221
The Korean Culture And Arts Foundation
Category: Art Gallery
Address: Sestiere Castello 1260
30122 Venezia Italy
Phone: +39 04 12770990

#222
Cooperative: Gondolieri Traghetto S.Lucia
Category: Boating, Public Transportation
Address: Sestiere S. Croce, 270/A
30135 Venezia Italy
Phone: +39 04 1718235

#223
Sestiere di Castello
Category: Landmark, Historical Buildings
Address: Campo San Zaccaria
30122 Venezia Italy

#224
Veneziana Motoscafi Societa Cooperativa
Category: Boating
Address: Sestiere S. Croce, 503
30135 Venezia Italy
Phone: +39 04 1716124

#225
Soprintendenza per I Beni Artistici e Storici di Venezia
Category: Museum
Address: Sestiere Cannaregio 3553
30131 Venezia Italy
Phone: +39 04 1720661

#226
Artlife For The World
Category: Leisure Center
Address: Via Sestiere Cannaregio, 6021
30121 Venezia Italy
Phone: +39 04 15209723

#227
ART
Category: Art Gallery
Address: Sestiere San Marco 3339
30124 Venezia Italy
Phone: +39 04 15281660

#228
Fitness Point
Category: Fitness & Instruction
Address: Sestiere Castello, 6141
30122 Venezia Italy
Phone: +39 04 15209246

#229
Bacci Gregorio
Category: Art Gallery
Address: Sestiere Dorsoduro 720B
30123 Venezia Italy
Phone: +39 04 15287934

#230
Associazione Scientifica Palazzo Cappello
Category: Leisure Center
Address: Sestiere Castello, 6391
30122 Venezia Italy
Phone: +39 04 15221307

#231
Chiese Cattoliche Parrocchiali San Maria del Rosario
Category: Museum, Church
Address: Sestiere Dorsoduro 917
30123 Venezia Italy
Phone: +39 04 15230625

#232
Associazione Sportivo Culturale Master Club
Category: Fitness & Instruction
Address: Sestiere Castello, 6576/E
30122 Venezia Italy
Phone: +39 04 15225128

#233
Rava' Tobia
Category: Art Gallery
Address: Sestiere Dorsoduro 2324
30123 Venezia Italy
Phone: +39 04 12750332

#234
Soc. Bocciofila S. Sebastiano
Category: Sports Club
Address: Via Sestiere Dorsoduro, 2371
30171 Venezia Italy
Phone: +39 04 12750315

#235
Federazioni: Italiana
Giuoco Calcio
Category: Sports Club
Address: Sestiere Castello, 6805/A
30122 Venezia Italy
Phone: +39 04 15286087

#236
Galleria Minima Degan Bruno
Category: Art Gallery
Address: Via Giuseppe Verdi, 68
30171 Venezia Italy
Phone: +39 04 1962964

#237
Gruppo Furlan Cinecity di G.
Category: Cinema
Address: Piazza Erminio Ferretto, 16
30174 Venezia Italy
Phone: +39 04 1988664

#238
Anffas di Venezia Onlus
Category: Leisure Center
Address: Sestiere Castello, 620
30122 Venezia Italy
Phone: +39 04 12413923

#239
Gruppo Furlan Cinecity di G.
Category: Cinema
Address: C. del Popolo, 30
30172 Venezia Italy
Phone: +39 04 1986722

#240
Anffas di Venezia Onlus
Category: Leisure Center
Address: Sestiere Cannaregio, 3144
30131 Venezia Italy
Phone: +39 04 1719020

#241
GIO Arte
Category: Art Gallery
Address: Via Filiasi Jacopo, 77
30174 Venezia Italy
Phone: +39 04 1988414

#242
Istituto Romeno di Cultura e Delle
Ricerche Umanistiche
Category: Leisure Center
Address: Sestiere Cannaregio, 2214
30131 Venezia Italy
Phone: +39 04 15242309

#243
Teatro Toniolo
Category: Opera & Ballet, Music Venues
Address: P.tta Battisti Cesare, 3
30174 Venezia Italy
Phone: +39 04 1971666

#244
Centro Internazionale per
La Ricerca Strumentale C.I.R.S.
Category: Leisure Center
Address: Sestiere Cannaregio, 3095
30121 Venezia Italy
Phone: +39 04 15240550

#245
Cinema DLF S.R.L. Dante
Category: Cinema
Address: Via Sernaglia, 12
30100 Venezia Italy
Phone: +39 04 15381655

#246
Diporto Velico Veneziano
Category: Sports Club
Address: Sestiere Castello, SNC
30122 Venezia Italy
Phone: +39 04 15231927

#247
Cinox Group International Trade
Category: Art Gallery
Address: Sestiere San Marco 79A
30124 Venezia Italy
Phone: +39 04 12412883

#248
Associazioni: Settemari
Category: Leisure Center
Address: Sestiere Cannaregio, 4701
30131 Venezia Italy
Phone: +39 04 15206708

#249
**Grafica Antica
di Manlio Penso &C**
Category: Art Gallery
Address: Sestiere San Marco 2089
30124 Venezia Italy
Phone: +39 04 15227199

#250
**Associazione Culturale
Italo-Tedesca**
Category: Leisure Center
Address: Sestiere Cannaregio, 4118
30131 Venezia Italy
Phone: +39 04 12410491

#251
**Istituto Ellenico di Studi Bizantini
e Post Bizantini**
Category: Museum
Address: Sestiere Castello 3412
30122 Venezia Italy
Phone: +39 04 15226581

#252
Cir.R.Bverde U.Sp.Alvisana
Category: Sports Club
Address: Sestiere Cannaregio, 3269
30131 Venezia Italy
Phone: +39 04 15240106

#253
La Galleria
Category: Art Gallery
Address: Sestiere San Marco 2566
30124 Venezia Italy
Phone: +39 04 15207415

#254
**Cooperative: Daniele Manin
FRA Gondolieri di Venezia**
Category: Boating
Address: Sestiere Cannaregio, 4199
30100 Venezia Italy
Phone: +39 04 15222844

#255
**Museo Diocesano D'arte
Sacra Sant' Apollonia**
Category: Museum
Address: Sestiere Castello 4312
30122 Venezia Italy
Phone: +39 04 15229166

#256
Dielleffe Scherma Venezia
Category: Sports Club
Address: Sestiere Cannaregio, 3163
30131 Venezia Italy
Phone: +39 04 1717960

#257
Progetto Venezia
Category: Art Gallery
Address: Sestiere San Marco 3201
30124 Venezia Italy
Phone: +39 04 15200673

#258
Associazione Sportiva Novafit
Category: Fitness & Instruction
Address: Sestiere Cannaregio, 5356
30131 Venezia Italy
Phone: +39 04 15228636

#259
Tornabuoni Arte
Category: Art Gallery
Address: Sestiere San Marco 2663
30124 Venezia Italy
Phone: +39 04 15231201

#260
Fita Venezia Ass. Culturale
Category: Leisure Center
Address: SRE Cannaregio, 483/B
30121 Venezia Italy
Phone: +39 04 10993768

#261
Ghidoli Giorgio
Category: Art Gallery
Address: Sestiere Castello 3472
30122 Venezia Italy
Phone: +39 04 15237590

#262
Ekos Club
Category: Leisure Center
Address: Isola Lazzareto Nuovo, 1
30100 Venezia Italy
Phone: +39 04 12444011

#263
Ikona Photo Gallery
Category: Art Gallery
Address: Sestiere Dorsoduro 48
30123 Venezia Italy
Phone: +39 04 15205854

#264
Prova D'artista
Category: Art Gallery
Address: Sestiere San Marco 1994B
30124 Venezia Italy
Phone: +39 04 15224812

#265
Tennis Canottieri Murano
Category: Sports Club
Address: Loc. Sacca S. Mattia, 1
30100 Venezia Italy
Phone: +39 04 1739592

#266
Round Midnight
Category: Opera & Ballet
Address: Sestiere Dorsoduro 3102
30123 Venezia Italy
Phone: +39 04 15232056

#267
**Associazione Culturale
Media Sound**
Category: Leisure Center
Address: Via dei Kirchmayr, 3/A
30100 Venezia Italy
Phone: +39 04 1770689

#268
**Soprintendenza per I Beni Artistici
e Storici di Venezia**
Category: Museum
Address: Sestiere Dorsoduro 1050
30123 Venezia Italy
Phone: +39 04 15212709

#269
Virtus Bocciofila Murano
Category: Sports Club
Address: Loc. Sacca S. Mattia,
30100 Venezia Italy
Phone: +39 04 1739294

#270
**V.A.V. Vence Arte Venezia
di Fornasier Giovanni**
Category: Art Gallery
Address: Sestiere SAN Polo,
30125 Venezia Italy
Phone: +39 04 15231108

#271
Palestra Club Delfino
Category: Gyms
Address: Dorsoduro 788/A
30123 VE Italy
Phone: +39 04 15232763

#272
Arcobaleno
Category: Arts & crafts
Address: Via Circonvallazione, 8
30171 Venezia Italy
Phone: +39 04 1986787

#273
**Barovier & Toso Vetrerie
Artistiche Riunite**
Category: Museum
Address: Fondamenta Vetrai 28
30141 Venezia Italy
Phone: +39 04 1739049

#274
Galleria D' Arte Contini
Category: Art Gallery
Address: Via Giorgio Ferro, 11
30174 Venezia Italy
Phone: +39 04 1980991

#275
Artitalia
Category: Art Gallery
Address: Sestiere San Marco 3627
30124 Venezia Italy
Phone: +39 04 15280203

#276
Caos Nicola
Category: Art Gallery
Address: Piazza San Marco 1047
30124 Venezia Italy
Phone: +39 04 12413561

#277
Cavallino Edizioni D'arte
di Paolo Cardazzo
Category: Art Gallery
Address: Sestiere Castello 5269A
30122 Venezia Italy
Phone: +39 04 15210488

#278
Cinema: Multisala Astra
Category: Cinema
Address: Via Corfu', 9
30126 Venezia Italy
Phone: +39 04 15265736

#279
Chiese Cattoliche Parrocchiali
San Zaccaria
Category: Museum, Church
Address: Sestiere Castello 4693
30122 Venezia Italy
Phone: +39 04 15221257

#280
Conservatorio di Musica
Benedetto Marcello
Category: Opera & Ballet, Musical
Instruments & Teachers, Music Venues
Address: Sestiere San Marco 2810
30124 Venezia Italy
Phone: +39 04 15225604

#281
Costantini Stefano Don
Category: Museum
Address: Via Sestiere Cannaregio 3282
30121 Venezia Italy
Phone: +39 04 15244664

#282
Galleria di Palazzo Cini
Category: Museum
Address: Sestiere Dorsoduro 864
30123 Venezia Italy
Phone: +39 04 15210755

#283
MAX Studio
Category: Art Gallery
Address: Sestiere Dorsoduro 1053C
30123 Venezia Italy
Phone: +39 04 15227773

#284
San Gregorio Art Gallery
Category: Art Gallery
Address: Sestiere Dorsoduro 164
30123 Venezia Italy
Phone: +39 04 15229296

#285
Schola San Zaccaria
Category: Art Gallery
Address: Via Castello 3456
30100 Venezia Italy
Phone: +39 04 15234343

#286
Soprintendenza per I Beni Artistici
e Storici di Venezia
Category: Museum
Address: Sestiere San Croce 2076
30135 Venezia Italy
Phone: +39 04 15241173

#287
Basilica Patriarcale di San Marco
Category: Museum, Church
Address: Sestiere San Marco 328
30124 Venezia Italy
Phone: +39 04 15225697

#288
Ghidoli Giuliana
Category: Art Gallery
Address: Sestiere Castello 3473
30122 Venezia Italy
Phone: +39 04 15203057

#289
Mazzucchi
Category: Art Gallery
Address: Sestiere San Marco 1771
30124 Venezia Italy
Phone: +39 04 15207045

#290
Soprintendenza Arch.per Il Veneto
e Friuli Venezia Giulia
Category: Museum
Address: Sestiere Cannaregio 5031
30131 Venezia Italy
Phone: +39 04 15200201

#291
Venice Design
Category: Art Gallery
Address: Sestiere San Marco 1310
30124 Venezia Italy
Phone: +39 04 15238530

#292
Musei Civici
Category: Museum
Address: Sestiere San Croce 2076
30135 Venezia Italy
Phone: +39 04 1721127

#293
Rai Radiotelevisione Italiana
Category: Museum
Address: Sestiere Cannaregio 275
30121 Venezia Italy
Phone: +39 04 1781111

#294
Abbazia Benedettina
Category: Museum, Church
Address: Isola San Giorgio Maggiore
30124 Venezia Italy
Phone: +39 04 15227827

#295
Alberghi: Hotel Hungaria Palace
Category: Opera & Ballet
Address: Granviale San Maria Elisabetta 28
30126 Venezia Italy
Phone: +39 04 12420060

#296
**B. & B. Art
di Bugno Massimiliano**
Category: Art Gallery
Address: Sestiere San Marco 1654
30124 Venezia Italy
Phone: +39 04 15288135

#297
Calzaturificio Donna Carolina
Category: Art Gallery
Address: Sestiere San Marco 1491
30124 Venezia Italy
Phone: +39 04 15225034

#298
**Cinema Multisala Giorgione Movie
D'essai**
Category: Cinema
Address: Sestiere Cannaregio 4612
30131 Venezia Italy
Phone: +39 04 15226298

#299
Collegio Armeno Moorat Raphael
Category: Museum
Address: Sestiere Dorsoduro 2596
30123 Venezia Italy
Phone: +39 04 15228770

#300
Ferruzzi Roberto
Category: Art Gallery
Address: Sestiere Dorsoduro 523
30123 Venezia Italy
Phone: +39 04 15228582

TOP 200 NIGHTLIFE

The Most Recommended by Locals & Trevelers

(From #1 to #200)

#1
Bacareto Da Lele
Category: Wine Bar
Address: Campo dei Tolentini 183
30135 Venezia Italy

#2
Taverna del Campiello Remer
Category: Jazz & Blues
Address: Cannaregio 5701
30125 Venezia Italy
Phone: +39 04 15228789

#3
Al Timon
Category: Bar, Italian
Address: Fondamenta degli Ormesini 2754
30121 Venezia Italy
Phone: +39 393 463209978

#4
Cantina Do Mori
Category: Wine Bar
Address: Sestiere San Polo 429
30125 Venezia Italy
Phone: +39 04 15225401

#5
Hard Rock Cafe Italy
Category: American, Bar
Address: Sestiere S. Marco, 1192
30124 Venezia Italy
Phone: +39 04 15229665

#6
Bar: Caffe' Florian - S.A.C.R.A.
Category: Bar
Address: Sestiere S. Marco, 56
30124 Venezia Italy
Phone: +39 04 15205641

#7
La Cantina
Category: Wine Bar
Address: Cannaregio 3689
30121 Venezia Italy

#8
Vino Vino
Category: Italian, Bar
Address: Ponte Delle Veste 2007A
30124 Venezia Italy
Phone: +39 04 12417688

#9
Birreria Forst
Category: Pub
Address: Calle delle Rasse 4540
30122 Venezia Italy
Phone: +39 04 15230557

#10
Harry's Bar
Category: Bar, Italian
Address: Sestiere San Marco 1323
30124 Venezia Italy
Phone: +39 04 15285777

#11
Osteria Alla Ciurma
Category: Wine Bar
Address: San Polo 406
30124 Venezia Italy
Phone: +39 340 6863561

#12
Enoteca Mascareta
Category: Wine Bar
Address: Calle lunga S.M.Formosa 5183
30122 Venezia Italy

#13
All'Amarone Vineria
Category: Wine Bar
Address: Calle dei Sbianchesini
30125 Venezia Italy
Phone: +39 04 15231184

#14
Corner Pub
Category: Pub
Address: Calle Della Chiesa
684 Venezia Italy
Phone: +39 03 299176561

#15
Devil Forest Pub
Category: Pub
Address: San Marco Venezia Italy
Phone: +39 04 15200623

#16
Osteria Alle Testiere
Category: Bar, Italian
Address: Sestiere Castello 5371
30122 Venezia Italy

#17
Ostaria al Ponte
Category: Italian, Pub
Address: Sestiere Cannaregio 6369
30121 Venezia Italy
Phone: +39 04 15286157

#18
Skyline Rooftop Bar
Category: Cocktail Bar
Address: Giudecca 810
30133 Venezia Italy
Phone: +39 04 12723311

#19
Orange
Category: Bar
Address: Campo Santa Margherita 3054A
30100 Venezia Italy
Phone: +39 415 234740

#20
Da Poggi
Category: Italian, Wine Bar
Address: Rio Terà de la Madalena 2103
30121 Venezia Italy
Phone: +39 04 1721199

#21
L'archivio
Category: Bar
Address: Sestiere di San Polo 256
30125 Venezia Italy
Phone: +39 04 12440132

#22
Blues Cafe
Category: Pub
Address: Dorsoduro N. 3778
30100 Venezia Italy
Phone: +39 03 954810275

#23
Al Marca
Category: Bar
Address: San Polo 213 Venezia Italy

#24
Angio'
Category: Bar
Address: Sestiere Castello, 2142
30122 Venezia Italy
Phone: +39 04 12778555

#25
Bar: Mirabar
Category: Bar
Address: Sestiere S. Croce, 555/A
30135 Venezia Italy
Phone: +39 04 15285218

#26
The Irish Pub
Category: Pub, Italian
Address: Sestiere Cannaregio
30121 Venezia Italy

#27
Caffe' Quadri
Category: Bar, Italian
Address: Sestiere San Marco 120
30124 Venezia Italy
Phone: +39 04 15222105

#28
Interpreti Veneziani
Category: Music Venues
Address: San Marco 2862B
30124 Venezia Italy
Phone: +39 04 12770561

#29
Torrefazione Marchi
Category: Bar
Address: cannaregio 1337
30121 Venezia Italy

#30
Antico Dolo
Category: Bar
Address: Ruga Vecchia San Giovanni 778
30125 Venezia Italy
Phone: +39 04 15226546

#31
San Vidal Snack Bar
Category: Bar
Address: Palazzo Loredan
30124 Venezia Italy
Phone: +39 04 15287843

#32
Foscarini
Category: Bar
Address: Sestiere Dorsoduro 878C
30123 Venezia Italy
Phone: +39 04 15227281

#33
Osteria del Cason
Category: Wine Bar, Seafood
Address: San Polo 2925
30125 Venezia Italy
Phone: +39 04 12440060

#34
Il Santo Bevitore
Category: Pub
Address: Cannaregio 2393A
30121 Venezia Italy
Phone: +39 335 8415771

#35
Bar: Al Nomboli
Category: Bar
Address: Sestiere SAN Polo, 2717/B
30125 Venezia Italy
Phone: +39 04 15230995

#36
Dogado Lounge
Category: Lounge
Address: Strada Nuova
30121 Venezia Italy
Phone: +39 04 15208544

#37
La Piscina
Category: Bar
Address: Sestiere Dorsoduro, 782
30123 Venezia Italy
Phone: +39 04 12413889

#38
Teamo
Category: Bar
Address: Calle Rio Terrà Mandola
30124 Venezia Italy
Phone: +39 347 3665016

#39
Bar Ducale
Category: Bar
Address: Sestiere S. Marco, 2354
30124 Venezia Italy
Phone: +39 04 15210002

#40
Muro Venezia Rialto
Category: Bar, Italian, Canteen
Address: San Polo 222
30135 Venezia Italy
Phone: +39 04 12412339

#41
BAR Rosa S.A.S.
Category: Bar
Address: Sestiere S. Croce, 1099
30135 Venezia Italy
Phone: +39 04 15200041

#42
Novecento
Category: Jazz & Blues
Address: Sestiere San Polo 900
30125 Venezia Italy
Phone: +39 04 15226565

#43
Enoteca Al Volto
Category: Wine Bar
Address: San Marco 4081 Venezia Italy
Phone: +39 04 15228945

#44
Margaret DuChamp
Category: Bar
Address: Campo Santa Margherita
30174 Venezia Italy

#45
Pizzeria Trattoria Vesuvio
Category: Bar, Italian
Address: Sestiere Cannaregio 1837
30121 Venezia Italy
Phone: +39 04 1795688

#46
Milo di Farag
Category: Pub, Cafe
Address: Dorsoduro 3684
30100 Venezia Italy

#47
BAR Cavatappi
Category: Bar, Italian
Address: Sestiere San Marco 525
30124 Venezia Italy
Phone: +39 04 12960252

#48
Bar: Snack BAR Nostro
Category: Bar
Address: Sestiere S. Marco, 5397
30124 Venezia Italy
Phone: +39 04 15237215

#49
Zanzibar
Category: Cafe, Bar
Address: Campo Santa Maria Formosa
30122 Venezia Italy
Phone: +39 347 1460107

#50
Caffe' del Doge
Category: Bar, Cafe
Address: Sestiere Castello 5197
30122 Venezia Italy
Phone: +39 04 12411949

#51
Bar alla Bragora
Category: Bar
Address: Castello 3604 Venezia Italy
Phone: +39 03 637110275

#52
Il Bar della Stazione
Category: Bar
Address: Stazione di Venezia Santa Lucia
30121 Venezia Italy

#53
Orange
Category: Bar
Address: SRE Dorsoduro, 3054
30100 Venezia Italy
Phone: +39 04 12414794

#54
Al paradiso perduto
Category: Music Venues
Address: Venezia Italy

#55
Ateneo di San Basso
Category: Music Venues
Address: Piazza San Marco
30124 Venezia Italy

#56
Poppa
Category: Cocktail Bar
Address: Sestiere Santa Croce
30135 Venezia Italy

#57
Cantina Vecia Carbonera
Category: Bar
Address: Strada Nova 2329
30121 Venezia Italy
Phone: +39 04 1710376

#58
Frulalà Fruit Bar
Category: Cocktail Bar
Address: Cannareggio 5620
Venezia Italy

#59
The Fiddlers Elbow
Category: Pub
Address: Campo già Testori
30121 Venezia Italy
Phone: +39 04 15239930

#60
Ca' Bonvicini
Category: Bar, Italian, Cafe
Address: Santa Croce
30124 Venezia Italy
Phone: +39 04 12750106

#61
Caffè alla Città di Torino
Category: Pizza, Bar
Address: Calle del Forno 4593
30124 Venezia Italy

#62
HK Venezia
Category: Italian, Wine Bar
Address: Sestiere di San Marco
30124 Venezia Italy
Phone: +39 04 12743614

#63
un mondo divino
Category: Wine Bar
Address: Salizada San Canciano
5984 Venezia Italy
Phone: +39 415 211093

#64
Bar Arsenale
Category: Pub
Address: Castello 2408 - Campo
dell'Arsenale Venezia Italy
Phone: +39 415 239913

#65
Bacaro Risorto
Category: Wine Bar, Cafe
Address: Campo San Provolo
4700 Venezia Italy
Phone: +39 04 15287274

#66
Raging Pub
Category: Pub
Address: Campo Santa Margherita
30123 Venezia Italy

#67
Osteria Blues Bar All'alba
Category: Jazz & Blues
Address: Sestiere San Marco 5370
30125 Venezia Italy

#68
Caffe' Chioggia
Category: Bar
Address: Sestiere S. Marco, 8/12
30124 Venezia Italy
Phone: +39 04 15237404

#69
Crazy Bar
Category: Pub
Address: Sestiere Castello 4972
30122 Venezia Italy

#70
Caffe' Bucintoro
Category: Bar
Address: Sestiere Castello, 4132
30122 Venezia Italy
Phone: +39 04 15285956

#71
Bar Karibu
Category: Bar
Address: Strada Castello 4682
30122 Venezia Italy
Phone: +39 04 10994620

#72
Inishark
Category: Irish, Pub
Address: Sestiere Castello 5787
30122 Venezia Italy
Phone: +39 04 15235300

#73
Osteria Al Bacareto
Category: Bar, Italian
Address: 3447 San Samuele
30124 Venezia Italy
Phone: +39 04 15289336

#74
Marciana
Category: Italian, Wine Bar
Address: Calle Larga San Marco 367 A
30124 Venezia Italy
Phone: +39 04 15206524

#75
BAR AL Campanile
Category: Bar
Address: Sestiere S. Marco, 310
30124 Venezia Italy
Phone: +39 04 15228678

#76
Al 133 Bar
Category: Bar
Address: Santa Croce 133
30135 Venezia Italy
Phone: +39 04 1713236

#77
Pizzeria Tre Archi
Category: Bar
Address: Via Cannaregio 552
30121 Venezia Italy
Phone: +39 04 1716438

#78
Da GIOSIA
Category: Wine Bar
Address: Santa Croce 458X
30135 Venezia Italy
Phone: +39 329 0771340

#79
Bar Al Car Can
Category: Bar, Cafe
Address: Via Santa Croce 133
30135 Venezia Italy
Phone: +39 04 1713236

#80
Hard Rock Café
Category: Pub
Address: Bacino Orseolo,
30124 Venezia Italy

#81
Barcollo
Category: Cocktail Bar
Address: Fondamenta Riva Olio
30125 Venezia Italy

#82
The Irish Pub Venezia
Category: Irish Pub
Address: Cannaregio 3847
30121 Venezia Italy
Phone: +39 04 10990196

#83
Caffè La serra
Category: Cocktail Bar
Address: via garibaldi 1254
30122 Venezia Italy

#84
BAR DA Gino
Category: Bar
Address: Sestiere Dorsoduro, 853/A
30123 Venezia Italy
Phone: +39 04 15285276

#85
Prendre Une Verre
Category: Bar
Address: calle dei fabbri 881
30124 Venezia Italy

#86
Snack BAR S. Vidal
di Bragato Lorenzo
Category: Bar
Address: Via S. Marco, 2862/A
30124 Venezia Italy
Phone: +39 04 15287843

#87
Zecchin / Valerio
Category: Bar
Address: Sestiere S. Marco, 3464
30124 Venezia Italy
Phone: +39 04 15220710

#88
BAR Cico BAR
Category: Bar
Address: Sestiere SAN Polo, 1960
30125 Venezia Italy
Phone: +39 04 1720603

#89
Saraceno S.A.S. di Lando Lino
& C. - Societa' IN
Category: Bar
Address: Sestiere SAN Polo, 726
30125 Venezia Italy
Phone: +39 04 15225556

#90
Al Prosecco
Category: Wine Bar
Address: Santa Croce 1503
30124 Venezia Italy

#91
Do Draghi
Category: Bar
Address: Dorsoduro 3665 Venezia Italy
Phone: +39 04 15289731

#92
Alberghi: Savoia Jolanda S.r.l.
Category: Bar, Italian
Address: Sestiere Castello 4187
30122 Venezia Italy

#93
BAR Trattoria AL Calinetto SAS
di Lazzarin G
Category: Bar
Address: Via Castello, 3803
30122 Venezia Italy
Phone: +39 04 15200776

#94
Da Nico
Category: Bar
Address: Campazzo dei Tolentini 191
30135 Venezia Italy

#95
Rustechi
Category: Italian, Bar
Address: Calle Farnese
30121 Venezia Italy

#96
Bar: Koko BAR
Category: Bar
Address: Sestiere S. Croce, 548/G
30135 Venezia Italy
Phone: +39 04 15200336

#97
Cambusa
Category: Pub
Address: Corte Mazor 2331-2333
30123 Venezia Italy

#98
Da Nini
Category: Bar
Address: Sestiere Cannaregio 1306
30131 Venezia Italy
Phone: +39 04 1717894

#99
Gran Caffe' Laguna
di Ursotti Giuseppe
Category: Bar
Address: PL. Della Colonna, 1
30141 Venezia Italy
Phone: +39 04 15274193

#100
Piccolo Mondo
Category: Dance Club
Address: Sestiere Dorsoduro, 1056/A
30123 Venezia Italy
Phone: +39 04 15200371

#101
Bar Internazionale
Category: Bar
Address: Riva degli Schiavoni
Venezia Italy

#102
Hosteria Al Rusteghi
Category: Italian, Wine Bar
Address: Sestiere San Marco 5529
30124 Venezia Italy
Phone: +39 04 15232205

#103
AL Verde
Category: Bar
Address: Sestiere Castello, 4526
30122 Venezia Italy
Phone: +39 04 15237094

#104
BAR Pasticceria Baldo Emilio
Category: Bar
Address: Via Castello, 1828
30122 Venezia Italy
Phone: +39 04 15232414

#105
Avvenire di Prevedello
Dellisanti Luciano
Category: Bar
Address: Via Dorsoduro, 3019
30123 Venezia Italy
Phone: +39 04 15286255

#106
Bar Aurora
Category: Bar
Address: Via Lungomare Trieste, 9,
33054 Venezia Italy

#107
BAR Chiaranda
di Vizza' Michela & C.snc
Category: Bar
Address: Piazza SAN Marco, 1165
30124 Venezia Italy
Phone: +39 04 15285228

#108
Chet Bar
Category: Lounge
Address: Dorsoduro 3684
30100 Venezia Italy

#109
Caffetteria Treponti
Category: Bar
Address: Sestiere Dorsoduro, 3502
30123 Venezia Italy
Phone: +39 04 15237257

#110
Si.Mi.
Category: Bar
Address: Sestiere Dorsoduro, 1191
30123 Venezia Italy
Phone: +39 04 15200196

#111
IDA BAR
Category: Bar
Address: Sestiere Dorsoduro, 2196
30123 Venezia Italy
Phone: +39 04 1713322

#112
BAR Caffe' Ca'foscari
Category: Bar
Address: Sestiere Dorsoduro, 3914
30100 Venezia Italy
Phone: +39 04 1710578

#113
Bar: AE Maraveje
Category: Bar
Address: Sestiere Dorsoduro, 1185
30123 Venezia Italy
Phone: +39 04 15235768

#114
Round Midnight
Category: Bar, Music Venues
Address: Sestiere Dorsoduro 3102
30123 Venezia Italy
Phone: +39 04 15232056

#115
**BAR S.Marta
di Zubiolo Maristella**
Category: Bar
Address: Sestiere Dorsoduro, 2126
30123 Venezia Italy
Phone: +39 04 15289492

#116
Susy di Granata Simone
Category: Bar
Address: Sestiere Dorsoduro, 1527
30123 Venezia Italy
Phone: +39 04 15227502

#117
Caffe' La Brasiliana
Category: Bar
Address: Sestiere S. Marco, 4986
30124 Venezia Italy
Phone: +39 04 15285774

#118
Osteria DA Carla di Menoghi
Category: Bar
Address: Sestiere S. Marco, 1535
30124 Venezia Italy
Phone: +39 04 15237855

#119
**Teatro Stabile del Veneto
Carlo Goldoni**
Category: Music Venues
Address: Sestiere S. Marco, 4650
30124 Venezia Italy
Phone: +39 04 12402011

#120
**Al Stagneri SNC di Marco Nordio
e Stefano Dall'agnola**
Category: Bar
Address: Sestiere S. Marco, 5246
30124 Venezia Italy
Phone: +39 04 15227341

#121
Bar: S. Marco
Category: Bar
Address: Sestiere S. Marco, 881
30124 Venezia Italy
Phone: +39 04 15237756

#122
Ilpi di Soranzo Pierluigi
Category: Bar
Address: Sestiere S. Marco, 3658/A
30124 Venezia Italy
Phone: +39 04 15239918

#123
Spaghetteria
Category: Bar
Address: Sestiere S. Marco, 2808
30124 Venezia Italy
Phone: +39 04 15203070

#124
BAR Mister Sandwich di Gue.ri
Category: Bar
Address: Sestiere SAN Marco, 5120/5121
30124 Venezia Italy
Phone: +39 04 15236086

#125
Ristorante Osteria N. 1
Category: Bar
Address: Sestiere S. Marco, 598
30124 Venezia Italy
Phone: +39 04 15226168

#126
Bar: Rizzo C. & G.
Category: Bar
Address: Sestiere S. Marco, 5125
30124 Venezia Italy
Phone: +39 04 15286304

#127
S.A.C.R.A.
Category: Bar
Address: Sestiere S. Marco, 1627/B
30124 Venezia Italy
Phone: +39 04 15284310

#128
Bar: Olimpia Sprint
Category: Bar
Address: Sestiere S. Marco, 1076
30124 Venezia Italy
Phone: +39 04 15225203

#129
Caffe' Gobbion
Category: Bar
Address: Sestiere S. Marco, 220
30124 Venezia Italy
Phone: +39 04 15237522

#130
**Conservatorio di Musica
Benedetto Marcello**
Category: Music Venues
Address: Sestiere San Marco 2810
30124 Venezia Italy
Phone: +39 04 15225604

#131
**Piramide dei F.lli Egiziani
di S. Wahba Guirgus**
Category: Bar
Address: Sestiere S. Marco, 355
30124 Venezia Italy
Phone: +39 04 12411380

#132
Rizzo G.& G.
Category: Bar
Address: Sestiere S. Marco, 933/A
30124 Venezia Italy
Phone: +39 04 15223388

#133
S.Y. S.N.C. di YU Xiaoyi
Category: Bar
Address: Sestiere S. Marco, 4717
30124 Venezia Italy
Phone: +39 04 15208085

#134
Teso / Mauro
Category: Bar
Address: Sestiere S. Marco, 1176
30124 Venezia Italy
Phone: +39 04 15235612

#135
Caffe dei Frari o Toppo
Category: Cafe, Dive Bar
Address: San Polo 2564 Fondamenta dei
Frari 30125 Venezia Italy
Phone: +39 04 15241877

#136
**BAR Lucano
di Zambon Danilo e Luigi**
Category: Bar
Address: Via SAN Marco, 480
30124 Venezia Italy
Phone: +39 04 15285294

#137
Lizhou HU Csnc
Category: Bar
Address: Via Cannaregio, 6140
30121 Venezia Italy
Phone: +39 04 12413685

#138
G.P.E. Gestione Pubblici Esercizi
Category: Bar
Address: Sestiere SAN Polo, 2807
30125 Venezia Italy
Phone: +39 04 15285150

#139
BAR Tris di Mancin Luigina
Category: Bar
Address: Sestiere SAN Polo, 476
30125 Venezia Italy
Phone: +39 04 15228841

#140
**Saraceno S.A.S.
di Lando Lino & C.**
Category: Bar
Address: Sestiere SAN Polo, 729
30125 Venezia Italy
Phone: +39 04 15210355

#141
BAR Quick Italy
Category: Bar
Address: Sestiere SAN Polo, 740
30125 Venezia Italy
Phone: +39 04 15226271

#142
Baristo
Category: Bar
Address: Sestiere SAN Polo, 3057
30125 Venezia Italy
Phone: +39 04 1713120

#143
BAR Stellina di YE JUN
Category: Bar
Address: Sestiere SAN Polo, 362
30125 Venezia Italy
Phone: +39 04 12960723

#144
Al Musicanti
Category: Bar
Address: Sestiere SAN Polo, 2580/A
30125 Venezia Italy
Phone: +39 04 12759264

#145
BAR Al Dieci Savi
Category: Bar
Address: Sestiere SAN Polo, 55
30125 Venezia Italy
Phone: +39 04 15238005

#146
**FAB 4 S.A.S di G.
Busana, A.targhetta**
Category: Bar
Address: Sestiere SAN Polo, 1105
30125 Venezia Italy
Phone: +39 04 15289224

#147
**Ristobar SAN Polo
di Zambon SAS**
Category: Bar
Address: Sestiere SAN Polo, 2024
30125 Venezia Italy
Phone: +39 04 15237218

#148
**Silver Star Snack BAR
di Centofanti Angelo**
Category: Bar
Address: Sestiere SAN Polo, 1857
30125 Venezia Italy
Phone: +39 04 12750777

#149
**Leone SNC di C.amedei
& Bruna Danuol**
Category: Bar
Address: Sestiere SAN Polo, 1131
30125 Venezia Italy
Phone: +39 04 15231184

#150
Campalto Aldo
Category: Bar
Address: Via Cannaregio, 2710
30100 Venezia Italy
Phone: +39 04 1715834

#151
Arcobaleno SAS di K. Sojer
Category: Bar
Address: Sestiere Castello, 3977
30122 Venezia Italy
Phone: +39 04 15229940

#152
BAR Al Greci
Category: Bar
Address: Sestiere Castello, 4988
30122 Venezia Italy
Phone: +39 04 15289780

#153
Cavallarin / Maurizia
Category: Bar
Address: Sestiere Castello, 4616
30122 Venezia Italy
Phone: +39 04 12412641

#154
**Clodia S.A.S. di Bullo Michael,
Barretta Antonio**
Category: Bar
Address: Sestiere Castello, 4590
30122 Venezia Italy
Phone: +39 04 15229324

#155
Luna S.N.C di Orlando Rizzo
Category: Bar
Address: Sestiere Castello, 4153
30122 Venezia Italy
Phone: +39 04 15212667

#156
Melodie Veneziane
Piccolo Teatro
Category: Dance Club
Address: Sestiere Castello, 5063/A
30122 Venezia Italy
Phone: +39 04 15231403

#157
BAR MIO
Category: Bar
Address: Sestiere Castello, 1820
30100 Venezia Italy
Phone: +39 04 15211361

#158
Osteria Al DO Pozzi DAI FIE
Category: Bar
Address: Sestiere Castello, 2613
30122 Venezia Italy
Phone: +39 04 15207141

#159
XU Biyu
Category: Bar
Address: Sestiere Castello, 1726
30122 Venezia Italy
Phone: +39 04 12412851

#160
Piccolo BAR
di Tagliapietra Giampaolo
Category: Bar
Address: Sestiere S. Croce, 2080
30135 Venezia Italy
Phone: +39 04 15241573

#161
Soprintendenza Beni Ambientali ED
Architettonici del Veneto
Category: Music Venues
Address: Sestiere S. Croce, 770
30135 Venezia Italy
Phone: +39 04 12574011

#162
Castellet / Antonio
Category: Bar
Address: Sestiere S. Croce, 2119
30135 Venezia Italy
Phone: +39 04 15240321

#163
Re del Tramezzino
Snack BAR di Piccin Elio
Category: Bar
Address: Sestiere Castello, 5354
30122 Venezia Italy
Phone: +39 04 15200765

#164
Blus BAR Della G & G S.N.C.
di Giuliana e Gabriella Rizzi
Category: Bar
Address: Sestiere Cannaregio, 4545
30121 Venezia Italy
Phone: +39 04 15289689

#165
Lizhou HU
Category: Bar
Address: Sestiere Cannaregio, 6140
30121 Venezia Italy
Phone: +39 04 12413685

#166
Baccio S.A.S. di Bacciolo Valter
Category: Bar
Address: Sestiere Cannaregio, 116
30121 Venezia Italy
Phone: +39 04 1715165

#167
Parolin / Bruno
Category: Bar
Address: Sestiere Cannaregio, 1102
30121 Venezia Italy
Phone: +39 04 1715077

#168
Doppiazeta S.N.C.
di Stefano e Luca Zane
Category: Bar
Address: Sestiere Cannaregio, 5042
30121 Venezia Italy
Phone: +39 04 15235687

#169
S.A.C.R.A.
Category: Bar
Address: Sestiere Castello, 5453
30122 Venezia Italy
Phone: +39 04 15220727

#170
Pullman BAR di Susino Maria
Category: Bar
Address: Sestiere S. Croce, 497
30135 Venezia Italy
Phone: +39 04 15230669

#171
Silvan BAR
Category: Bar
Address: Sestiere S. Croce, 187/A
30135 Venezia Italy
Phone: +39 04 1710112

#172
Marti's BAR di Martignon Fabio
Category: Bar
Address: Sestiere Castello, 5619
30122 Venezia Italy
Phone: +39 04 15285296

#173
Taverna 'Olandese Volante'
Category: Bar
Address: Sestiere Castello, 5658
30122 Venezia Italy
Phone: +39 04 15289349

#174
Baccio
Category: Bar
Address: Via Sestiere Canareggio, 116
30121 Venezia Italy
Phone: +39 04 1715165

#175
BAR IN Campieo SNC
di Brocchetto Gianfranco
Category: Bar
Address: Via S. Croce, 24
30135 Venezia Italy
Phone: +39 04 1711061

#176
Fabris / Daniela
Category: Bar
Address: Sestiere S. Croce, 97
30135 Venezia Italy
Phone: +39 04 1715236

#177
Desmo SNC
di Marangoni Gabriele
Category: Bar
Address: Sestiere S. Croce, 453
30135 Venezia Italy
Phone: +39 04 15206293

#178
IDA BAR
Category: Bar
Address: Sestiere Castello, 6778
30122 Venezia Italy
Phone: +39 04 12770483

#179
BAR Colleoni di Vianello G.
Category: Bar
Address: Via Castello, 6810
30122 Venezia Italy
Phone: +39 04 15224967

#180
BAR Cometa SNC di Jiang C.
Category: Bar
Address: Via Castello, 538
30122 Venezia Italy
Phone: +39 04 15284666

#181
Snack BAR La Tazza D'oro
Category: Bar
Address: SRE Castello, 4864
30122 Venezia Italy
Phone: +39 04 15227716

#182
Buffet Stazione Venezia
Category: Bar
Address: Sestiere Cannaregio, 44/45
30131 Venezia Italy
Phone: +39 04 1715097

#183
Ass. Culturale Vortice
Category: Music Venues
Address: Sestiere Cannaregio, 5013
30131 Venezia Italy
Phone: +39 04 12412156

#184
Fratelli Salin di Matteo Salin
Category: Bar
Address: Sestiere Cannaregio, 376
30131 Venezia Italy
Phone: +39 04 1716037

#185
Torrefazione Marchi
Category: Bar
Address: Sestiere Cannaregio, 1337
30100 Venezia Italy
Phone: +39 04 1710471

#186
**BAR Cristallo SNC
di F. & O. Cacco**
Category: Bar
Address: Sestiere Cannaregio, 321
30131 Venezia Italy
Phone: +39 04 1716507

#187
Lazzarini Manuel e Gianluca
Category: Bar
Address: Sestiere Cannaregio, 6370
30131 Venezia Italy
Phone: +39 04 15285783

#188
Nuova Valiglia
Category: Italian, Wine Bar
Address: San Marco 4697
30124 Venezia Italy
Phone: +39 04 15226330

#189
Enobar
Category: Bar
Address: Salizada San Giovanni Grisostomo
Venezia Italy

#190
Bar: Filovia
Category: Bar
Address: Sestiere S. Croce, 521/A
30135 Venezia Italy
Phone: +39 04 15236051

#191
X.j.di YU Xiao YI & NI JIN Xian
Category: Bar
Address: SRE S. Polo, 1697
30100 Venezia Italy
Phone: +39 04 10993682

#192
Venetian Navigator 2
Category: Bar
Address: SRE Castello, 5300
30100 Venezia Italy
Phone: +39 04 12771056

#193
AL Pontile di Costantini Sebastiano
Category: Bar
Address: Sestiere S. Martino Sinistra, 834
30012 Venezia Italy
Phone: +39 04 1730055

#194
La Parmigiana di LU Jianping
Category: Bar
Address: Place Parmesan, 1
30100 Venezia Italy
Phone: +39 04 1929525

#195
Zennaro / Gino
Category: Bar
Address: Str. Casa Rossa, 18
30100 Venezia Italy
Phone: +39 04 1731080

#196
BAR AL Turista
Category: Bar
Address: Sestiere S. Martino Destra, 14/A
30012 Venezia Italy
Phone: +39 04 1735670

#197
Bacaro Jazz
Category: Jazz & Blues, Italian
Address: Salizada del Fontego dei Tedeschi
5546 30124 Venice Italy
Phone: +39 04 15285249

#198
Pizzeria da Sandro
Category: Bar, Pizza
Address: Via San Polo 1473
30125 Venezia Italy
Phone: +39 04 15234894

#199
Marcianavenice
Category: Wine Bar, Italian
Address: Calle Larga Santa Marca 367 A
30124 Venezia Italy
Phone: +39 04 15206524

#200
Ostaria Dai Zemei
Category: Pub
Address: Sestiere San Polo 1045
30125 Venezia Italy
Phone: +39 04 15208596

Made in the USA
San Bernardino, CA
15 April 2018